DUTCH

MADE EASY LEVEL 1

An Easy Step-By-Step Approach
To Learn Dutch for Beginners
(Textbook + Workbook Included)

Lingo Mastery

ISBN: 978-1-951949-74-7

The illustrations in this book were designed using images from Freepik.com.

CONTENTS

PREFACE / ABOUT DUTCH

A foreign language is an essential means of communication in modern times, both for business or for social goals, such as traveling or migrating.

Dutch is the third most spoken West Germanic language (after German and English). Today, there are more than 24 million Dutch speakers worldwide for whom Dutch is the first language. The total number of Dutch speakers worldwide makes Dutch one of the 40 most widely spoken languages in the world.

Here are some facts about this wonderful language:

- Dutch is the official language of the Netherlands (17 million speakers), of Suriname (600,000 speakers), and one of the three official languages of Belgium (6.5 million speakers).
- Within the Kingdom of the Netherlands, Dutch is also an official language of the Caribbean islands of Aruba, Curaçao, and Sint Maarten.
- In the former colony of Indonesia, the oldest generations may still speak Dutch in some areas. The number of speakers of Dutch (mainly immigrants) in the United States, Canada, and Australia is estimated at more than half a million.
- Afrikaans, one of the official languages of South Africa, is a daughter language of Dutch and both languages are mutually intelligible.
- In the European Union, about 23 million people speak Dutch as their first language and another eight million as their second language.

To learn a new language, it is important to have good learning resources, and books are one of the best materials – they are essential tools to achieve our goals. It is important to find the right resource, and you need one that best suits your needs and goals. Apart from the content, the book should also be attractive and have a clear design.

This is what we offer you with this **Dutch Vocabulary Workbook**.

STRUCTURE

There are efficient methods that allow you to learn Dutch in a self-taught and independent way. These methods include complete support materials designed to approach Dutch in all its aspects: written and oral comprehension and written and oral expressions. A good method allows you to make progress in Dutch while having fun. The method will, ideally, simulate real-life situations. If you want to learn to communicate in Dutch quickly, this is the book for you!

This book will introduce you to the Dutch language in a solid and effective way, teaching you the linguistic, cultural, and strategic tools to communicate and to keep progressing. This self-study tool will focus on the formal aspects of the language only as they relate to how the language is used. You will learn important concepts for the use of verbs in Dutch.

This book has ten units with lessons on spelling, phonetics, vocabulary, everyday expressions, grammar, and many exercises to practice oral and written comprehension. The teaching sequence has been carefully planned so that you can gain experience in using the language, using the context over everyday situations like going grocery shopping, asking for directions, and going to see the doctor.

The activities are selected to reinforce communicative, linguistic, thematic, and learning domains. They include dialogues, texts, cultural and linguistic information to strengthen your knowledge of the language.

If you want to go to the next level in conversation, reading, and writing, this book is the one for you!

INTRODUCTION

The pedagogical approach of this book is based on a vision of language as a site of interaction, as a mediating dimension of the relationships established between subjects and different cultural worlds. Language is not just a form or system, but a set of possibilities for interaction and experience that includes not only formal structures and their rules, but also all the social, cultural, historical, and political meanings that make it up.

Learning Dutch means gaining cultural and linguistic experiences in a new language, reflecting on that language and your own mother tongue. It also means considering you as an active subject. It prepares you to interact in Dutch in everyday situations in different contexts.

Reasons to study and learn Dutch include the ability to communicate with Dutch speakers in your community, make your travel experiences more rewarding and exciting, increase your job opportunities, improve, and better understand your own language, and enjoy Dutch music, literature, movies, and theatre in the language they were created in.

RECOMMENDATIONS

The book covers levels up to A2 in the Common European Framework of Reference for Languages (CEFR). At this level, the language learner can understand and use familiar everyday expressions and basic phrases aimed at satisfying concrete needs. The student can introduce him/herself to others and can ask and answer questions about personal details such as where he/she lives, people he/she knows, and things he/she owns. The student can answer in a simple way, assuming the other person speaks slowly and clearly and is willing to help (source: Common European Framework of Reference for Languages (CEFR), 2001).

The **Dutch Made Easy Level 1** workbook is an excellent tool for anyone motivated to learn Dutch by themselves. Here are some general recommendations and tips:

- Mistakes happen: We all make mistakes, especially when learning a new language, but that should not discourage you; on the contrary, it should encourage you to learn from your mistakes. It shows you are brave and capable of learning and applying new things outside your comfort zone, even when you know it is not perfect yet.

- Dutch pronunciation can be a bit daunting at first with its myriad of vowel sounds and guttural g that you might not be used to. Our advice is to really take your time with the audio files, listen to them and repeat them several times until those sounds start rolling off your tongue more naturally.

- There is no need to rush because every person has his/her own pace. Take your time; eventually you will learn everything. And please, do not feel frustrated or disappointed if there are concepts or units that take more time than others.

- Finally, practice makes perfect!

This headphone symbol beside the heading of a text, dialogue or exercise indicates that audio content is available for the corresponding section.

This headphone with a pencil next to an exercise means that you will need to refer to the corresponding audio content to complete the exercise.

Throughout the book we have included info-boxes with additional content, tips, and recommendations:

INTERESSANTE WEETJES

Facts and explanations about culture and language use in the Netherlands and Belgium.

LEERTIPS

Useful tips and recommendations for learning Dutch.

SUPPLEMENTARY VOCABULARY SETS...

...are presented in these colors and help you increase the number of things you can say and write as you study each unit.

They may appear alongside the grammatical explanations within a section or as part of the vocabulary list at the end of a section. They sometimes contain additional word lists sorted by topic or a set of useful phrases, depending on context.

GRAMMAR OVERVIEW TABLES...

...are presented in these colors and contain concise grammatical overviews, often supplemented with example sentences and expressions.

HOW TO GET THE AUDIO FILES

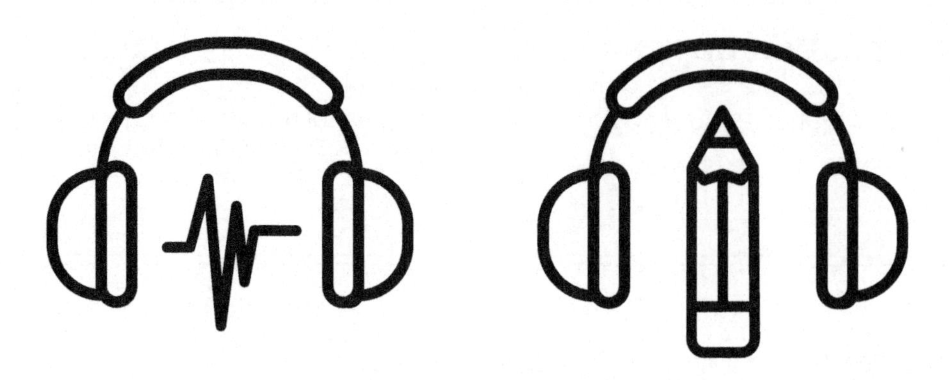

Some of the exercises throughout this book come with accompanying audio files.
You can download these audio files if you head over to:
www.lingomastery.com/dutch-me1-audio

Basisbeginselen
The basics

1
Deel
Unit

Unit 1 focuses on introducing a few basic questions and answers, numbers from 0 to 10, family members, and extensively covers Dutch pronunciation which you will practice with several listening exercises.

VOCABULARY	PRONUNCIATION
- Introducing yourself - Numbers from 0-10 - Family members	- All the letters in the alphabet, as well as vowel combinations.

1.1 DUTCH IN CONTEXT: HOE HEET JIJ?

WHAT'S YOUR NAME?

TRACK 1 Three people, Annemieke, Dirk and Gijs, meet for the first time at a volleyball club. Listen to their conversation and read along. (Find audio on page 6.)

Annemieke: *Goedemorgen! Is dit zaal 5? Ik zit in groep 3B.*

Dirk: *Goedemorgen! Ja, dit is zaal 5. Ik zit ook in groep 3B. Ik heet Dirk, en jij?*

Annemieke: *Ik heet Annemieke. Aangenaam kennis met je te maken!*

Dirk: *Aangenaam!*

Gijs: *Hallo, is dit zaal 5? Ik zoek volleybal groep 3B.*

Annemieke: *Ja, groep 3B traint hier. Ik ben nieuw.*

Gijs: *Ik ben ook nieuw! Ik ben Gijs.*

Annemieke: *Ik ben Annemieke en dit is Dirk.*

Gijs: *Aangenaam! Oh, het is 10 uur, de training begint nu!*

Useful phrases from the conversation:

Goedemorgen! Is dit zaal 5? → *Good morning! Is this training hall 5?*

Ik zit in groep 3B. → *I'm in group 3B.*

Ik heet Dirk, en jij? → *My name is Dirk, and yours?*

Aangenaam kennis met je te maken! → *Pleased to meet you!*

Ik zoek volleybal groep 3B. → *I'm looking for volleyball group 3B.*

Ik ben nieuw. → *I'm new.*

Ik ben Annemieke en dit is Dirk. → *I'm Annemiek and this is Dirk.*

Oh, het is 10 uur. De training begint nu! → *Oh, it's ten o'clock. The training starts now!*

TRACK 2 You already heard a few numbers in the conversation. So let's learn the numbers from 0 to 10. Listen to the audio to learn the correct pronunciation. (Find audio on page 6.)

0	1	2	3	4	5	6	7	8	9	10
nul	één	twee	drie	vier	vijf	zes	zeven	acht	negen	tien

DUTCH IN CONTEXT: MIJN FAMILIE MY FAMILY

 **TRACK 3** The image below shows a portrait of Piet's family. Listen to him describing the photo and read along. (Find audio on page 6.)

Piets familie:
Vader Kees, dochter Lianne, vrouw Hanneke, zoon Jelle, dochter Belle, Piet, zoon Jip en moeder Miep.

Ik ben Piet. Ik ben getrouwd en ik heb vier kinderen, twee zonen en twee dochters. Ik heb geen ooms en tantes. Mijn ouders zijn dol op al hun kleinkinderen!

INTERESSANTE WEETJES

You can see from the vocabulary list on the following page that Dutch makes no difference between cousin and niece/nephew. Similarly, vrouw means wife but also woman in general, and man means husband but also man in general. If you're ever unsure about who someone is referring to, just ask them to clarify.

FAMILIE (FAMILY)	
Dutch	**English**
(de) vader	father
(de) papa	dad
(de) moeder	mother
(de) mama	mom
(de) ouders	parents
(de) broer	brother
(de) zus	sister
(de) opa	grandfather
(de) oma	grandmother
(de) tante	aunt
(de) oom	uncle
(de) neef	cousin, the nephew
(de) nicht	cousin, the niece
(de) vrouw	wife (also woman)
(de) man	husband (also man)
(de) zoon	son
(de) dochter	daughter
(het) kind	child
(het) kleinkind	grandchild

Useful phrases from the text:

Ik ben getrouwd. → I'm married.

Ik heb geen ooms en tantes. → I don't have any uncles and aunts.

Mijn ouders zijn dol op al hun kleinkinderen. → My parents adore all their grandchildren.

1.2 UITSPRAAK

PRONUNCIATION

The Dutch alphabet, like the English alphabet, is a Latin alphabet with 26 letters and about 40 sounds. The 20 Dutch consonants are generally pronounced very similarly to their English counterparts. The alphabet contains the same 5 vowels as in English, but their sound is usually shorter. There are short vowel sounds, long vowel sounds, and combinations of sounds (diphthongs) in Dutch. A diphthong (*tweeklank*) is a sound formed by combining two vowels in one syllable. The difference between short vowels and long vowels is critical for a very important spelling/grammar rule which affects many nouns and verbs, which we will explain later in Unit 3.

TRACK 4 The table below lists the letter, its International Phonetic Alphabet (IPA) symbol, example words with the letter in English, and a further explanation. Listen to the audio to hear the letter the way it's pronounced in the alphabet and all the Dutch example words. (Find audio on page 6.)

LETTER	IPA	EXAMPLES	FURTHER EXPLANATION AND SIMILAR SOUND IN AN ENGLISH WORD
A (short)	/ɑ/	*man* (man) *bak* (storage bin) *kast* (closet)	Similar to the *a* in "hard" or "party", but shorter.
B	/b/	*bank* (couch) *web* (spiderweb)	Very similar to the English *b*. but when it's at the end of a word (web) it sounds more like a soft *p*.
C	/c/ before e, i /k/ before a, o, u	*centrum* (center) *circus* (circus) *cursus* (course)	When the *c* comes before an *a*, *o* or *u*, the sound is similar to an English *k* or *c* (like in the word cat), but without the release of air which is so typical for the English *k*.
D	/d/	*dag* (day) *doen* (to do) *rood* (red) *dood* (dead)	When the *d* is at the beginning or in the middle of a word, it's similar to the English *d*, but without the release of air. However, when the *d* is at the end of a word, its sound is closer to a *t* in English.
E (short)	/ɛ/ /ə/	*lek* (leak) *plek* (place) *de* (the)	The Dutch short *e* is similar to the *e* in "set" but shorter. In many words, especially at the end of the word, the e is just like the English schwa-sound (like in the unstressed version of the article "the").
F	/f/	*fles* (bottle) *verf* (paint)	Practically the same as the English *f*.
G	/x/	*gek* (crazy) *genoeg* (enough)	This guttural *g* does not exist in English. The closest similar sound would be the *ch* in the Scottish word "loch".
H	/ɦ/	*hallo* (hello) *behalve* (except)	Practically the same as the English *h*.

I (short)	/ɪ/	*lip* (lip) *begin* (start)	The same as the short *i* in English in words like "sit", "in", "with".
J	/j/	*ja* (yes) *meisje* (girl)	The Dutch *j* sounds like the *y* in English, like in "yard", "yoga", "you".
K	/k/	*kaars* (candle) *buik* (tummy)	The Dutch *k* is similar to the English *k*, but without the release of air which is so typical for the English *k*.
L	/l/	*laag* (low) *smal* (narrow)	Practically the same as the English *l*.
M	/m/	*moeder* (mother) *maan* (moon)	Practically the same as the English *m*.
N	/n/	*nieuw* (new) *pen* (pen)	Practically the same as the English *n*.
O (short)	/ɔ/	*kom* (bowl) *zon* (sun)	Very similar to the short *o* in English in words like "on", "of", "stop", but shorter.
P	/p/	*pop* (doll) *plank* (shelf)	The Dutch *p* is similar to the English *p*, but without the release of air which is so typical for the English *p*.
Q	/q/	*quiche* (quiche)	The Dutch *q* is similar to the English *q*, but without the release of air which is so typical for the English *q*.
R	/r/	*radio* (radio) *broer* (brother)	There's no English equivalent sound. The Dutch is made by trilling the tongue in the back of the mouth.
S	/s/	*slang* (snake) *huis* (house)	Practically the same as the English *s*.
T	/t/	*tomaat* (tomato) *tante* (aunt)	The Dutch *t* is similar to the English *t*, but without the release of air which is so typical for the English *t*.
U (short)	/ʏ/	*nummer* (number) *zus* (sister)	There's no exact equivalent in English, it's roughly like the *u* in "nurse" and "purse".
V	/v/	*vis* (fish) *vader* (father)	The Dutch *v* sounds a bit more like an English *f*.

W	/ʋ/	*wit* (white) *waar* (where) *jouw* (your)	When the *w* is at the start of the word, it sounds more like an English *v*, but without the release of air used in English. When the *w* is in any part of the word, its sound is like the *w* in "view".
X	/ks/	*extra* (extra) *xenofobie* (xenophobia)	Practically the same as the English *x*, with a 'ks' sound, in "extra".
Y	/j/ /iː/	*yoghurt* (yogurt) *typen* (to type)	When it's the first letter of the word, it sounds like the English *y* in "yoga". But if it's used as a vowel, like in the word *typen*, it sounds like the double *e* in "beetle".
Z	/z/	*zebra* (zebra) *verzoek* (request)	Practically the same as the English *z*.

TRACK 5 Dutch is famous for its large number of words with double vowels and diphthongs. The table below lists them the vowel combinations with examples and further notes about their pronunciation. Listen to the audio to hear the letter the way it's pronounced in the alphabet and all of the Dutch example words. (Find audio on page 6.)

SOUND COMBINATIONS	IPA	EXAMPLES	FURTHER EXPLANATION AND SIMILAR SOUND IN AN ENGLISH WORD
aa (long)	/a/	*maan* (moon)	Somewhat similar to the *a* in father, but longer. It's also similar to the second *a* in Hawaii.
ee (long)	/eɪ/	*beek* (brook) *veel* (a lot)	Exactly like the '*a*' or '*ea*' in the English words "cake", "take", "steak".
oo (long)	/oʊ/	*droog* (dry) *oom* (uncle)	Exactly like the *o* in the English words "know", "joke".
uu (long)	/y/	*vuur* (fire) *duur* (expensive)	Roughly like the English diphthong *ew* like in the words "few", "pew".

au, ou	/ʌu/	*blauw (*blue*)* *koud* (cold)	Similar to the English diphthong /aʊ/ like in the words "shout", "mouth".
ei, ij	/ɛi/	*trein* (train) *ei* (egg) *fijn* (nice)	There's no exact equivalent in English, it's somewhat similar to the vowel sound in "might", "high" but pronounced with the mouth more like a smile.
eu	/ø:/	*neus* (nose) *deur* (door)	There's no exact equivalent in English, it's somewhat similar to the vowel sound in "fur", "dirt", but more drawn out.
ie (long i)	/i/	*riet* (reed) *tien* (ten)	Very similar to the diphthongs in "street", "beach", "feet", but less drawn out.
oe	/u/	*hoed* (hat) *doen* (to do)	Similar to the vowel sounds in "rule", "fool".
ui	/œy/	*tuin* (garden) *huis* (house)	There's no exact equivalent in English, but it's quite similar to the Scottish pronunciation of the word "house".
uw	/yu/	*duw* (push) *ruw* (rough)	It's quite similar to the vowel sounds in the words "new", "pew", "few".
ch	/x/	*licht (*light*)* *nicht* (female cousin and niece)	This guttural g sound does not exist in English. The closest similar sound would be the *ch* in the Scottish word "loch".
sch*	/sx/	*schip (*ship) *schoon (*clean)	There's no exact equivalent in English, the sound is created by combining the *s* and the guttural *g*.
aai/ooi/oei	/a:i/ /o:i/ /ui/	*saai (*boring) *mooi* (beautiful) *doei* (bye)	The *aai* sound is quite similar to the vowel sound in high, but longer. The *ooi* sound is similar to the vowel sound in boy, but longer. The *oei* sound is similar to the vowel sound you get when saying *two weeks*.
eeuw/ieuw	/e:u/ /iu/	*leeuw (*lion*)* *nieuw (*new*)*	There are no equivalent sounds in English to *eeuw*, but *nieuw* sounds quite similar to new.

1.3 OEFENINGEN
EXERCISES

TRACK 6 1) Mastering that Dutch pronunciation: In the audio you will hear the words from the table below with vowels, vowel combinations and consonant sounds that don't have an equivalent sound in English. Listen carefully and repeat the words. (All answers to the exercises are found in the answer key starting from page 123) (Find audio on page 6.)

	Sound	Dutch	English
1	aa	*maan*	moon (n)
2	uu	*duur*	expensive (adj)
3	auw	*pauw*	peacock (n)
4	ei	*klein*	small (adj)
5	eu	*neus*	nose (n)
6	ouw	*mouw*	sleeve (n)
7	ui	*ruit*	window, diamond (shape) (n)
8	uw	*sluw*	sly (adj)
9	ij	*pijn*	pain (n)
10	ch	*nicht*	cousin, niece (n)
11	sch	*schoen*	shoe (n)

TRACK 7 2) Words with the short a: On the tape, you will hear the words with the short a from the table below. Listen carefully and repeat the words: (Find audio on page 6.)

	Dutch	English
1	*pan*	pan (n)
2	*kam*	comb (n)
3	*dam*	dam (n)
4	*lang*	long (adj)
5	*kast*	closet (n)

TRACK 8 3) Words with the short e: On the tape, you will hear the words with the short e from the table below. Listen carefully and repeat the words: (Find audio on page 6.)

	Dutch	English
1	*pen*	pen (n)
2	*klem*	clip (n), stuck (adj)
3	*merk*	brand (n)
4	*stem*	voice (n)
5	*pet*	cap (n)

TRACK 9 4) Words with the short i: On the tape, you, will hear the words with the short i from the table below. Listen carefully and repeat the words: (Find audio on page 6.)

	Dutch	English
1	*stip*	dot (n)
2	*gil*	scream (n)
3	*stil*	silent (adj)
4	*bril*	glasses (n)
5	*willen*	to want (v)

TRACK 10 5) Words with the short o: On the tape, you will hear the words with the short o from the table below. Listen carefully and repeat the words: (Find audio on page 6.)

	Dutch	English
1	*kom*	bowl (n)
2	*tor*	beetle (n)
3	*rok*	skirt (n)
4	*kort*	short (adj)
5	*bord*	plate (n)

TRACK 11 6) Words with the short u: On the tape, you will hear the words from the table below with words with the short u. Listen carefully and repeat the words: (Find audio on page 6.)

	Dutch	English
1	*rug*	back (n)
2	*stuk*	broken (adj), a piece (n)
3	*put*	well (n)
4	*club*	club (n)
5	*bus*	bus (n)

TRACK 12 7) Choose the correct word: On the tape you will hear one of the words from the 3 options presented. Listen carefully and select the word you hear. The first one has already been filled out as an example. (Find audio on page 6.)

	Option A:	Option B:	Option C:
1	***pen***	*pin*	*pan*
2	*ach*	*oog*	*och*
3	*deur*	*duur*	*daar*
4	*peen*	*poen*	*pijn*
5	*bas*	*bus*	*bos*
6	*doen*	*dun*	*dan*
7	*luw*	*leeuw*	*lauw*
8	*tien*	*tin*	*ten*

8) Family members: This is Ellen's family tree. Complete the sentences below with the correct family member in Dutch which you learned in vocabulary section 1 of this unit. The first one has already been filled out as an example.

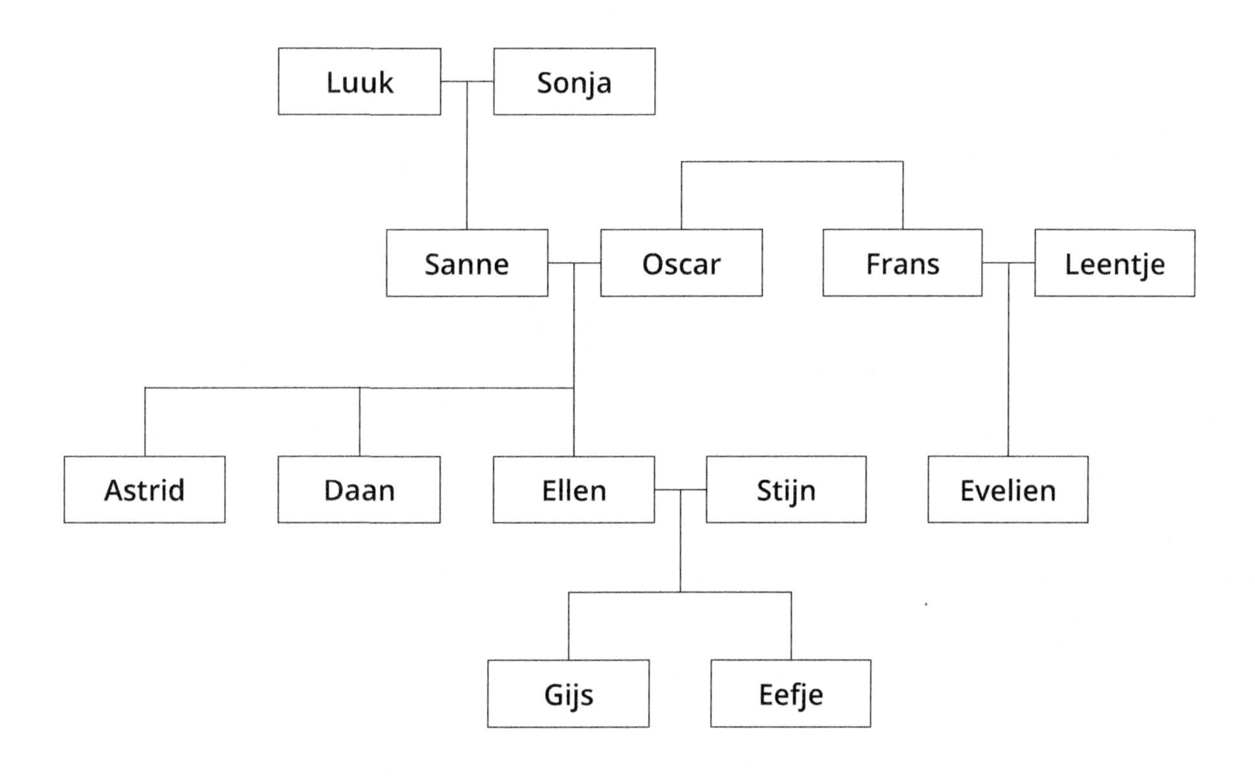

1) Gijs is mijn ______**zoon**______.

2) Evelien is mijn ____________________.

3) Astrid is mijn ____________________.

4) Eefje is mijn ____________________.

5) Stijn is mijn ____________________.

6) Sonja is mijn ____________________.

7) Daan is mijn ____________________.

8) Luuk is mijn ____________________.

9) Sanne is mijn ____________________.

10) Frans is mijn ____________________.

11) Leentje is mijn ____________________.

1.4 WOORDENLIJST
VOCABULARY LIST

goedemorgen	good morning
(de) bak	storage bin
(de) bank	couch, bank
(de) bril	pair of glasses
(de) buik	stomach
(de) cursus	course
(de) dag	day
(de) dam	dam
(de) deur	door
(de) duw	push
(de) fles	bottle
(de) gil	scream
(de) hoed	hat
(de) kaars	candle
(de) kast	closet
(de) kom	bowl
(de) leeuw	lion
(de) maan	moon
(de) neus	nose
(de) pan	pan
(de) pauw	peacock
(de) pen	pen
(de) pet	cap
(de) plank	plank, shelf
(de) plek	place
(de) pop	doll
(de) rok	skirt
(de) rug	back
(de) schoen	shoe

(de) slang	snake, hose
(de) stem	voice, vote
(de) stip	dot
(de) tomaat	tomato
(de) tor	beetle
(de) tuin	garden
(de) verf	paint
(de) vis	fish
(de) zon	sun
(het) bord	plate, traffic sign
(het) ei	egg
(het) huis	house
(het) lek	leak
(het) licht	light
(het) meisje	girl
(het) merk	brand
(het) schip	ship
(het) vuur	fire
aangenaam	it's a pleasure to meet you
beginnen	to start
behalve	except
ben	am
de	the
doen	to do
dol zijn op	to adore somebody, to adore something
droog	dry
duur	expensive
fijn	nice
gaan	to go
gek	crazy
genoeg	enough
getrouwd	married

hallo	hello
ik	I
ja	yes
jij	you
jouw	your
klein	small
koud	cold
laag	low
lang	long, tall
mooi	pretty, beautiful
nu	now
rood	red
saai	boring
schoon	clean
smal	narrow
stil	quiet
stuk	broken, piece
veel	a lot (of)
waar	where, true
willen	to want
wit	white

Nieuwe mensen ontmoeten

Meeting new people

2

Deel

Unit

Unit 2 focuses on introducing the vocabulary and grammar for common questions and answers you will need when meeting new people. This includes common greetings, talking about where you're from, and professions.

VOCABULARY	GRAMMAR
- Personal pronouns - Common greetings - Meeting people for the first time - Common professions - Countries and nationalities	- Conjugation of seven common verbs in the present tense - Definite and indefinite articles

2.1 DUTCH IN CONTEXT: WAAR KOM JE VANDAAN?

WHERE ARE YOU FROM?

TRACK 13 Johan and Lonneke are a couple that meets Tina and Patrick at their first university class. Listen to their conversation and read along.

Johan: *Goedemorgen. Is dit de geschiedenisles?*

Tina: *Ja! Goedemorgen. Ik heet Tina, en jij?*

Johan: *Ik heet Johan, en dit is mijn vriendin Lonneke. Aangenaam kennis met je te maken.*

Lonneke: *Hoi Tina. Waar kom je vandaan?*

Tina: *Ik kom uit Schiedam, en jullie?*

Lonneke: *Ik kom uit Utrecht en Johan komt uit Groningen.*

Tina: *Leuk! Hey, daar komt Patrick.*

Patrick: *Ehm, hallo. Hoe heet jij?*

Johan: *Ik heet Johan. En waar kom jij vandaan?*

Patrick: *Ik kom uit Engeland.*

Johan: *Interessant!*

Tina: *De les begint, ssh!*

Useful phrases from the conversation:

Questions:

Hoe heet jij? → What's your name?

Waar kom je vandaan? → Where are you from?

Answers:

Ik heet Tina, en jij? → My name's Tina, and yours?

Ik kom uit Engeland. → I'm from England.

FORMELE EN INFORMELE BEGROETINGEN (FORMAL AND INFORMAL GREETINGS)	
Formal:	
goededag	good day
goedemorgen	good morning
goedemiddag	good afternoon
goedenavond	good evening
hallo	hello
tot ziens	goodbye
Informal:	
hoi	hi
dag, doei, doeg	bye

Namen van landen en nationaliteiten **(Names of countries and nationalities)**

Nederland
Nederlands

Canada
Canadees

Amerika/De VS
Amerikaans

Groot-Brittannië
Brits

Marokko
Marokkaans

Oekraïne
Oekraïens

Duitsland
Duits

Japan
Japans

Australië
Australisch

Spanje
Spaans

Brazilië
Braziliaans

Frankrijk
Frans

Denemarken
Deens

Zweden
Zweeds

Zuid-Afrika
Zuid-Afrikaans

Argentinië
Argentijns

Mexico
Mexicaans

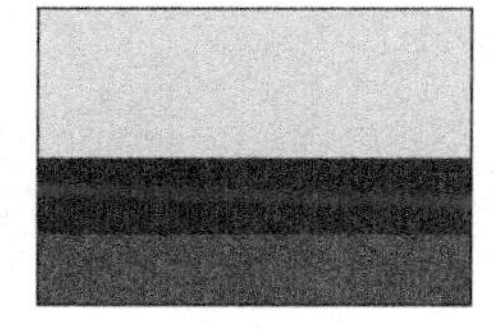
Colombia
Colombiaans

China
Chinees

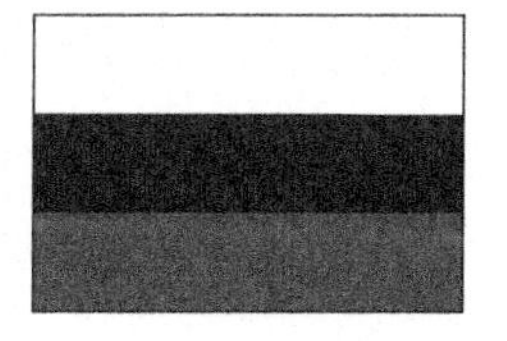
Rusland
Russisch

Let's meet a few people:

	Ik heet Anne Kronstadt. *Ik kom uit Zweden.* *Ik ben Zweeds.*	My name is Anne Kronstadt. I'm from Sweden. I'm Swedish.

	Ik heet John McLellan. *Ik kom uit Canada.* *Ik ben Canadees.*	My name is John McLellan. I'm from Canada. I'm Canadian.

Now practice how to say your name and where you're from:

Ik heet ______________. *Ik kom uit* ______________. *Ik ben* ______________.

DUTCH IN CONTEXT: WAT VOOR WERK DOE JE? WHAT DO YOU DO?

TRACK 14 Petra, Leo and Kina are former high school classmates that meet at a school reunion after 20 years. Listen to their conversation and read along.

Petra: *Hoi, ben jij Leo?*

Leo: *Ja! Petra? Hey, hoe gaat het?*

Petra: *Heel goed! En met jou?*

Leo: *Ook goed! Vertel, wat voor werk doe je?*

Petra: *Ik ben accountant. En jij?*

Leo: *Ik ben arts. Ik werk in het Deventer Ziekenhuis.*

Petra: *Interessant! Hey! Kina?*

Kina: *Ja, ik ben Kina! Petra?*

Petra: *Ja! Dit is Leo, hij is arts, interessant hè!*

Kina: *Zeker! Ik ben lerares op een middelbare school. En waar werk jij?*

Petra: *Ik ben accountant en ik werk bij een supermarkt.*

Kina: *Super!*

Useful phrases from the conversation:

Questions:

Hoe gaat het? → How are you?

Vertel, wat is je beroep?
→ Tell me, what's your profession?

Waar werk je? → Where do you work?

Answers:

Heel goed. → Very well.

Ik ben winkelmedewerker.
→ I'm a shop assistant.

Ik werk in het ziekenhuis. → I work at the hospital.

Zeker! → Definitely!

BEROEPEN (PROFESSIONS)			
Dutch	English	Dutch	English
(de) dokter/arts	doctor/physician	*(de) elektricien*	electrician
(de) verpleger (m), verpleegster (v)	nurse (m/f)	*(de) ingenieur*	engineer
(de) leraar (m), lerares (v)	teacher (m/f)	*(de) advocaat*	lawyer
(de) wetenschapper	scientist	*(de) bouwvakker*	construction worker
(de) politicus	politician	*(de) winkelmedewerker*	shop assistant
(de) softwareontwikkelaar	software designer	*(de) student*	student
(de) accountant	accountant	*(de) architect*	architect
(de) kok	chef	*(de) kunstenaar, artiest*	artist
(de) timmerman	carpenter	*(de) vertaler*	translator

LEERTIPS

Make use of modern technology for your Dutch learning journey as much as you can: find videos on YouTube, podcasts and short stories online. Try to find topics you find interesting in your own language; this will really help your motivation.

2.2 GRAMMAR: WERKWOORDEN IN DE ONVOLTOOID TEGENWOORDIGE TIJD

VERBS IN THE PRESENT SIMPLE

Before we delve into conjugation, it's important to understand two basic concepts about verbs in Dutch: how to recognize the **infinitive form** and the **stem** of the verb.

1. The infinitive form of the verb ends in *-en* (for example, *werken*) which would be the equivalent of "to work" in English. The exception to the rule of infinitives always ending in -en are these 5 monosyllabic verbs that end in -n, without the e (*gaan, staan, slaan, doen, zien*), but we'll look at those in another unit.
2. The stem of the verb is found by removing the -en from the infinitive. Therefore, the stem of the verb *werken*, is *werk*.

In the table below, we'll present the conjugation of two regular verbs and illustrate this rule.

		CONJUGATION OF EXAMPLE VERBS		CONJUGATION RULE FOR REGULAR VERBS
PERSONAL PRONOUN		*Werken (to work)*	*Komen (to come)*	*Infinitive of the verb: stem + en*
ik	I	*werk*	*kom*	stem
Je (jij), u	you	werk***t***	kom***t***	stem + **t**
hij, ze (zij), het	he, she, it	werk***t***	kom***t***	stem + **t**
We (wij)	we	*werken*	*komen*	Infinitive
jullie	you	*werken*	*komen*	Infinitive
ze (zij)	they	*werken*	*komen*	Infinitive

Notes on the conjugation:

As the table illustrates, the conjugation for first-person singular (*ik*) is the same as the stem (*werk*). The conjugation for the 2nd and 3rd person singular (*jij, u, hij, zij, het*) is formed by adding a *-t* to the stem (*werkt*). The conjugation of the verbs for all plural pronouns is always the same as the infinitive.

Notes on the pronouns:

1. *Je, we* and *ze* have the same meaning as *jij, wij* and *zij*, respectively. *Je, we* and *ze* are used in sentences where the pronoun isn't stressed. For example: *Je hebt een hond* and *jij hebt een hond* both mean "you have a dog", but in the latter the stress of the sentence would be placed on *jij*.

2. Careful with ze (zij), it means both she (singular) and they (plural)!

3. *U* is the formal way of *je, jij* in singular and of *jullie* in plural (2nd person). It's used in writing and when you speak to elderly people or in a formal setting (business) and to people you're talking to for the first time. However, nowadays it's becoming more and more common to use the informal form *je* or *jij*. When used in plural the conjugation is still in singular.

Irregular verbs:

Unfortunately, not all verbs are as regular as *werken*. In the table below, we'll present two very common verbs that are irregular (*zijn* and *hebben*).

		IRREGULAR VERBS	
PERSONAL PRONOUN		***Zijn (to be)***	***Hebben (to have)***
ik	I	*ben*	*heb*
*Je (jij), u**	you	*bent*	*hebt*
hij, ze (zij), het	he, she, it	*is*	*heeft*
We (wij)	we	*zijn*	*hebben*
jullie	you	*zijn*	*hebben*
ze (zij)	they	*zijn*	*hebben*

*The formal second-person pronoun *u* can be used in the singular and plural but generally follows the conjugation of *je*. With the verb *hebben*, however, it's more common to say *u heeft*, following the conjugation of third person singular.

Verbs with a vowel added to the stem:

To understand the rules that apply to a very large group of Dutch verbs, it's important to understand the concept of **open and closed syllables**. We'll illustrate this by using the verbs *hebben* (to have) and *heten* (to be called) as examples.

1. When splitting the verb *hebben* into two syllables, we get *heb-* and *ben*. These would both be considered closed syllables since they end in a consonant.

2. When splitting the verb *heten* into two syllables, we get *he-* and *ten*. The first syllable, *he*, would be considered an open syllable since it ends in a vowel.

Why is this distinction important? Open syllables often use the "long" pronunciation of the vowel, which is invariably the same sound as the double vowel. This means that the pronunciation of the "o" in the verb *lopen*, is actually the same in the singular (*loop/loopt*) and the plural (*lopen*). Despite the spelling being different, both are pronounced like the o in go.

In the table below, we'll present you with three very common verbs where a vowel is added to the stem in the conjugation for singular pronouns.

		VERBS WITH A VOWEL ADDED TO THE STEM		
PERSONAL PRONOUN		*weten (to know)*	*lopen (to walk)*	*vragen (to ask)*
ik	I	*weet*	*loop*	*vraag*
Je (jij), u	you	*weet*	*loopt*	*vraagt*
hij, ze (zij), het	he, she, it	*weet*	*loopt*	*vraagt*
We (wij)	we	*weten*	*lopen*	*vragen*
jullie	you	*weten*	*lopen*	*vragen*
ze (zij)	they	*weten*	*lopen*	*vragen*

Usage of the *onvoltooid tegenwoordige tijd* (present simple) in Dutch:

Now that you know how to conjugate a few verbs in Dutch, let's talk about what the tense known as *onvoltooid tegenwoordige tijd* is used for. Its usage is a lot broader than the present simple in English.

Here's a summary:

1. To refer to a temporary action happening at the time of speaking, where we often use the present continuous in English.

   Example: *Het sneeuwt.* (It's snowing.)

2. To refer to a continuous, habitual, or repetitive action or state, where we would often use the present perfect in English.

   Example: *Ze woont in Delft.*
   (She's living/lives in Delft.)

3. To refer to a future event, where we often use a future tense or expression in English.

   Example: *We gaan morgen naar het park.* (We're going to the park tomorrow.)

4. To refer to a hypothetical "if – then" situation, where we would use "will" for the result clause in English.

   Example: *Als je veel oefent, leer je snel Nederlands.*
   (If you practice a lot, you will learn Dutch quickly.)

GRAMMAR: LIDWOORDEN DEFINITE AND INDEFINITE ARTICLES

Since we use articles to precede nouns in most cases, it's important to get them right from the start. Dutch has only one indefinite article, but two definite articles.

Indefinite article (only used for singular nouns):

Een → a, an

Definite articles:

De and *het* → the

De is the article used for singular nouns considered gendered (male or female) and *het* is the article used for singular nouns considered neuter nouns. That being said, it is still really a case of slowly learning the article for each new word that you learn because the gender of nouns isn't referred to in any other way in Dutch. The good news is that the article is always *de* if nouns are plural.

Examples:

De scholier → The student

De scholieren → The students

Het boek → The book

De boeken → The books

LEERTIPS

Like English, Dutch also has the schwa sound (/ə/ in the phonetic alphabet), and it is very common. The article *de* is a word that uses this vowel sound, and when verbs are used in their infinitive or plural, ending in *-en*, the vowel sound is also schwa.

2.3 OEFENINGEN
EXERCISES

1) Look at the information about the person in the image and write their name, where they're from, and what their profession is (in first person). The first one has been filled out as an example.

1) Angela Ponti / Italië / scholier	Ik heet Angela Ponti. Ik kom uit Italië. Ik ben scholier.
2) Marc Smith / Groot-Brittannië / ingenieur	
3) Johann Schmitt / Duitsland / politicus	
4) Yanet Sanchez / Spanje / lerares	

2) Choose the correct verb from the two options to match the pronoun used in the sentence.
The first one has been filled out as an example.

1) Jij (**heet**/loopt) Gert Zeegers.

2) Ik (heet/kom) uit Nederland.

3) Hij (is/komt) timmerman.

4) We (hebben/komen) een tuin.

5) Zij (heet/hebt) Tina Jansen.

6) Jullie (heten/vragen) mijn naam.

7) Zij (komen/lopen) uit de Verenigde Staten.

8) Wij (hebben/zijn) scholieren.

9) U (bent/heet) wetenschapper.

3) Choose the correct verb conjugation from the options given:

1) Jullie (werk/werkt/werken) op de universiteit.

2) U (heet/heten) Lonneke Verheijen. (remember: U is singular)

3) Isabel (kom/komt/komen) uit de Verenigde Staten.

4) We (loop/loopt/lopen) naar de les.

5) De vertaler (vraag/vraagt/vragen) naar het boek.

6) Jullie (ben/bent/is/zijn) Duits.

7) Het boek (heet/heten) *'De Avonden'*.

8) Ik (ben/bent/is/zijn) leraar.

TRACK 15 4) Definite articles: The articles (*de* or *het*) are missing from the short sentences below. Listen carefully to the tape and fill in the blanks with the articles. The first one has been filled out as an example.

1) Dit is ___**het**___ ziekenhuis. (This is the hospital.)

2) ___________ bouwvakkers werken. (The construction workers are working.)

3) ___________ geschiedenisles is saai. (The history lesson is boring.)

4) ___________ licht is aan. (The light is on.)

5) ___________ werkwoorden zijn moeilijk. (The verbs are difficult.)

5) Writing about yourself: Complete the following sentences with information about yourself. Use a dictionary if you need vocabulary that hasn't been introduced yet.

1) Ik heet ____.

2) Ik ben ____.
(Complete with your profession)

3) Ik kom uit ____.
(Complete with your country of origin)

4) Ik werk voor ____.
(Complete with the name of the company you work for)

2.4 WOORDENLIJST
VOCABULARY LIST

(de) accountant	accountant
(de) advocaat	lawyer
(de) architect	architect
(de) kunstenaar, artiest	artist
(de) bouwvakker	construction worker
(de) chef	chef
(de) leraar, lerares	teacher
(de) dokter/arts	doctor/physician
(de) elektricien	electrician
(de) ingenieur	engineer
(de) les	lesson
(de) politicus	politician
(de) scholier	student
(de) softwareontwikkelaar	software designer
(de) timmerman	carpenter
(de) verpleger, verpleegster	nurse
(de) vertaler	translator
(de) vriendin	female friend, girlfriend
(de) wetenschapper	scientist
(de) winkelassistent	shop assistant
(het) beroep	profession
(het) boek	book
(het) licht	light
(het) werkwoord	verb
(het) ziekenhuis	hospital
Amerikaans	American
Argentijns	Argentinian
Argentinië	Argentina
Australië	Australia

Australisch	Australian
Braziliaans	Brazilian
Brazilië	Brazil
Brits	British
Canadees	Canadian
Chinees	Chinese
Colombiaans	Colombian
De Verenigde Staten	The United States
Deens	Danish
Denemarken	Denmark
dag, doei, doeg	bye
Duits	German
Duitsland	Germany
een	a/an
Frankrijk	France
Frans	French
goededag	good day
goedemiddag	good afternoon
goedemorgen	good morning
goedenavond	good evening
Groot-Brittannië	Great Britain
hebben	to have
het	it, the
hij	he
hoe	how
hoi	hi
tot ziens	goodbye
interessant	interesting
Japans	Japanese
jij/je	you (singular)
jullie	you (plural)
komen	to come

lopen	to walk
Marokkaans	Moroccan
Marokko	Morocco
Mexicaans	Mexican
Mexico	Mexico
moeilijk	difficult
Nederland	The Netherlands
Nederlands	Dutch
oefenen	to practice
Oekraïens	Ukrainian
Oekraïne	Ukraine
Rusland	Russia
Russisch	Russian
Spaans	Spanish
Spanje	Spain
vragen	to ask
we (wij)	we
werken	to work
weten	to know
wonen	to live
ze (zij)	she, they, them
zijn	to be
Zuid-Afrika	South Africa
Zuid-Afrikaans	South African
Zweden	Sweden
Zweeds	Swedish

In de stad
In the city

3
Deel
Unit

Unit 3 focuses on giving you the vocabulary you'll need to find your way around a city, including names of places in a city, the prepositions of place, and common phrases used to ask for and give directions. You'll also learn how to form the plural of nouns, and learn the grammar behind the formation of questions in the present simple.

VOCABULARY	GRAMMAR
- Vehicles - Places in a city - Prepositions of place - Asking for and giving directions - Question words	- Conjugation of questions in the present simple - The impersonal *Er is / er zijn* (There is / there are) - Formation of nouns in the plural

3.1 DUTCH IN CONTEXT: HOE GA JE NAAR JE WERK?

HOW DO YOU GET TO WORK?

TRACK 16 Karel, Paula and Piet introduce themselves and tell us where they work and how they get to their place of work. Listen tot heir conversation and read along.

Karel: *Hallo! Ik heet Karel. Ik ben timmerman. Ik werk in Rotterdam, maar ik woon in Dordrecht. Ik ga met de trein naar mijn werk.*

Paula: *Goeiemorgen. Ik ben Paula. Ik ben tandarts. Ik woon en werk in Breda. Ik heb een auto, maar ik fiets naar mijn werk.*

Piet: *Hoi. Mijn naam is Piet. Ik ben softwareontwikkelaar. Ik woon in Groningen. Ik werk thuis. Ik heb een motor en daarmee ga ik naar de supermarkt.*

Useful phrases from the conversation:

Ik werk in Rotterdam, maar ik woon in Dordrecht. → I work in Rotterdam, but I live in Dordrecht.

Ik ga met de trein naar mijn werk. → I take the train to work.

Ik heb een auto, maar ik fiets naar mijn werk. → I have a car, but I cycle to work.

Ik werk thuis. → I work from home.

VOERTUIGEN (VEHICLES)	
Dutch	**English**
(de) fiets	bicycle
(de) voetganger	pedestrian
(de) auto	car
(de) bus	bus
(de) taxi	taxi
(de) motor	motorcycle
(de) trein	train
(de) tram	tram
(de) vrachtauto / vrachtwagen	truck
(het) openbaar vervoer	public transport

Before we move on to the next conversation, let's learn some basic prepositions of place and the names of some common places in the city.

VOORZETSELS VAN PLAATS (PREPOSITIONS OF PLACE)			
in (inside)	*onder* (under)	*tegenover* (opposite)	*op (on)*
voor (in front of)	*naast* (next to)	*dichtbij* (near)	*achter* (behind)

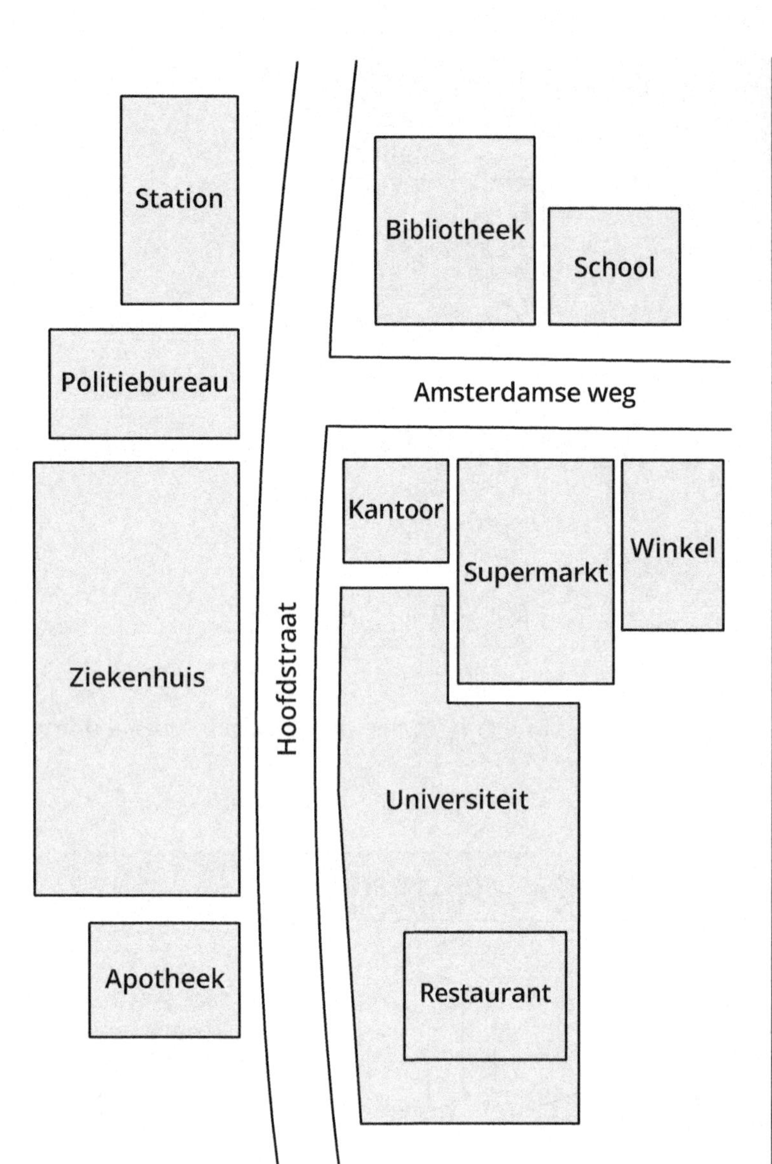

PLAATSEN IN DE STAD (PLACES IN A CITY)	
Dutch	**English**
(het) vliegveld	airport
(de) haven	port
(het) station	railway station
(het) kantoor	office
(de) winkel	shop
(het) plein	main square
(de) supermarkt	supermarket
(het) ziekenhuis	hospital
(de) apotheek	pharmacy
(het) zwembad	swimming pool
(de) sporthal	sports hall
(het) politiebureau	police station
(de) bibliotheek	library
(de) school	school
(de) universiteit	university
(het) restaurant	restaurant
(de) weg	road
(de) hoofdstraat	main street

Example phrases about the map:

De bibliotheek is naast de school. → The library is next to the school.

Het station is tegenover de bibliotheek. → The train station is opposite the library.

Het politiebureau is naast het ziekenhuis. → The police station is next to the hospital.

De universiteit is achter de supermarkt. → The university is behind the supermarket.

Het kantoor is dichtbij het politiebureau. → The office is close to the police station.

De winkel is tegenover de school. → The shop is opposite the school.

Er is een restaurant in de universiteit. → There is a restaurant inside the university.

DUTCH IN CONTEXT: WAAR IS DE SCHOOL? WHERE IS THE SCHOOL?

TRACK 17 Karel, Paula and Piet will now ask about the location of a place or directions to that place, based on the city map. Listen to the conversations and read along.

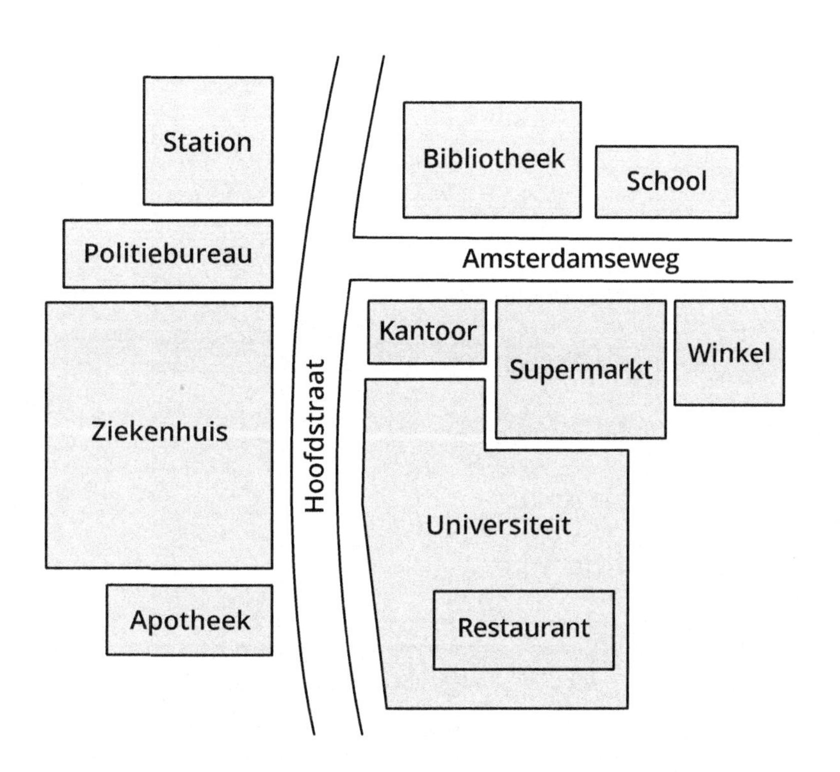

Karel: *Goedemiddag. Waar is de school?*

Politieman: *Goedemiddag meneer. De school is aan de Amsterdamseweg, naast de bibliotheek. Het is hier dichtbij.*

Karel: *Hartelijk bedankt!*

Piet: *Hallo. Ik ben verdwaald. Hoe kom ik bij de apotheek vanaf de winkel?*

Vrouw: *Hallo. Het is niet ver. Loop rechtdoor tot de Hoofdstraat, sla linksaf en loop langs het ziekenhuis. De apotheek zit naast de linkerkant van het ziekenhuis.*

Piet: *Bedankt mevrouw! Fijne dag verder.*

Paula: *Hey Hanneke. Is er hier een geldautomaat?*

Hanneke: *Ik weet het niet zeker. Misschien in de supermarkt, tegenover de bibliotheek.*

Paula: *Oké, bedankt!*

Useful phrases from the conversation:

Questions:

Waar is de school? → Where is the school?

Hoe kom ik bij de apotheek vanaf de winkel? → How do I get to the pharmacy from the shop?

Is er hier een geldautomaat? → Is there an ATM here?

Answers:

De school is aan de Amsterdamseweg, naast de bibliotheek. → The school is located on the Amsterdamseweg, next to the library.

(Hartelijk) bedankt. → Thank you (kindly).

Ik ben verdwaald. → I'm lost.

Fijne dag verder. → Have a great day.

Ik weet het niet zeker. → I'm not sure.

AANWIJZINGEN GEVEN EN BEGRIJPEN (GIVING AND UNDERSTANDING DIRECTIONS)	
Dutch	**English**
links	left
sla links af	turn left
rechts	right
sla rechts af	turn right
rechtdoor	straight ahead
tot, totaan	until
langs	past
aan de linkerkant	on the left-hand side
aan de rechterkant	on the right-hand side
loop	walk
neem	take
sla af	turn
hoek	corner
hier	here
daar	there
ver	far
dichtbij	close

3.2 GRAMMAR: MEERVOUD VAN ZELFSTANDIGE NAAMWOORDEN

NOUN PLURALS

There are quite a few things to take into account when forming noun plurals in Dutch, mostly in terms of spelling changes, that's why we've organized all these rules in groups.

These are the three ways of forming noun plurals in Dutch.

1. **Adding -en to the singular noun.** Examples: *fiets / fietsen* (bicycle, bicycles) and *tuin / tuinen* (garden, gardens). This is by far the most common way to form plurals. However, there are several spelling changes to consider when forming the plural this way.

   a. For nouns that end in a double vowel plus a consonant in their singular form (oo, ee, aa, uu + consonant): remove one of the vowels in the plural. Examples: *school / scholen* (school, schools) and *apotheek / apotheken* (pharmacy, pharmacies).

   b. For nouns that end in a/e/i/o/u plus a consonant in their singular form: duplicate the consonant in the plural. Examples: *bed / bedden* (bed, beds) and *bus / bussen* (bus, buses).

   c. For nouns that end in s, change this s for a z in the plural. Examples: *huis / huizen* (house, houses). Also, for nouns that end in f, change this f for a v in the plural. Example: *neef / neven* (cousin/nephew, cousins/nephews).

2. **Adding -s or -'s** to the singular noun. These are the categories of nouns that take an -s or -'s in the plural.

   a. Nouns ending in: -e, -eau, -ef, -el, -em, -en, -er, -ie, or -je. Examples: *winkel, winkels* (store, stores), *politiebureau, politiebureaus* (police station, police stations), *meisje, meisjes* (girl, girls) and *situatie, situaties* (situation, situations).

   b. Most nouns ending in an unstressed vowel. Examples: *tante, tantes* (aunt, aunts).

   c. Most foreign words (usually English or French). Examples: *tram, trams* (tram, trams).

   d. Nouns ending in -i, -a, -o, -u or -y. This is where you have to add an apostrophe before the s. Examples: *baby, baby's* (baby, babies) and *auto, auto's* (car, cars), *villa, villa's* (villa, villas).

3. **Adding -eren** to the singular noun. This is a very small group. The most common nouns that follow this rule are:

    a. *Blad / bladeren* (leaf, leaves), *kind / kinderen* (child, children), *ei / eieren* (egg, eggs) and *lied / liederen* (song, songs)

Remember that the definitive article for singular nouns is either *de* or *het*, but for plural nouns it is always *de*. Examples: *Het zwembad / de zwembaden* and *het meisje / de meisjes*.

GRAMMAR: VRAGEN IN DE TEGENWOORDIGE TIJD QUESTIONS USING THE PRESENT SIMPLE

In Unit 2 you've learned how to form affirmative sentences in the *tegenwoordige tijd*, now it's time to learn how to form questions in the same tense. These questions are used for the present and often also the immediate future. The basic rule is similar to how we form questions with the verb "to be" in English; inverting the subject/pronoun with the verb. Dutch does not use an auxiliary verb as English does.

Please note that for the second person singular (*jij/je*), you must remove the -t from the verb when forming the question. In the table below, we'll present you with the affirmative and question versions of verbs useful for the topic of getting around a city.

FIETSEN (TO CYCLE)		ZOEKEN (TO LOOK FOR)	
Affirmative	Question	Affirmative	Question
Ik fiets	*Fiets ik?*	*Ik zoek*	*Zoek ik?*
Jij fietst	*Fiets jij?*	*Jij zoekt*	*Zoek jij?*
Hij/zij/u fietst	*Fietst hij/zij/u?*	*Hij/zij/u zoekt*	*Zoekt hij/zij/u?*
Wij fietsen	*Fietsen wij?*	*Wij zoeken*	*Zoeken wij?*
Jullie fietsen	*Fietsen jullie?*	*Jullie zoeken*	*Zoeken jullie?*
Zij fietsen	*Fietsen zij?*	*Zij zoeken*	*Zoeken zij?*

Let's add the question words, so you can ask all the questions you'll ever want. The grammar box contains the main question words you'll need, have a look at the examples below. We've focused the examples on questions related to finding your way around a city.

Waar is de apotheek? → Where is the pharmacy?

Wat zoekt u? → What are you looking for?

Wie is de gids? → Who is the tour guide?

Waarom is de bus vol? → Why is the bus full?

Wanneer gaat de winkel open? → When does the shop open?

Hoeveel kost het kaartje? → How much does the ticket cost?

Hoe kom ik bij het plein? → How do I get to the main square?

VRAAGWOORDEN (QUESTION WORDS)	
Dutch	**English**
waar	where
wat	what
wie	who
waarom	why
wanneer	when
welk(e)	which
hoe	how
hoeveel	how much/many

GRAMMAR: ER IS / ER ZIJN THERE IS / THERE ARE

Just like in English, Dutch also has an impersonal expression which means "there is / there are". Note that when you use the plural, you usually don't need to use a definite or indefinite article.

Singular: *Er is* (there is)

Er is een vliegveld.

Er is een trein.

Is er een ziekenhuis?

Is er een busstation?

Plural: *Er zijn* (there are)

Er zijn vliegvelden.

Er zijn treinen.

Zijn er ziekenhuizen?

Zijn er busstations?

3.3 OEFENINGEN
EXERCISES

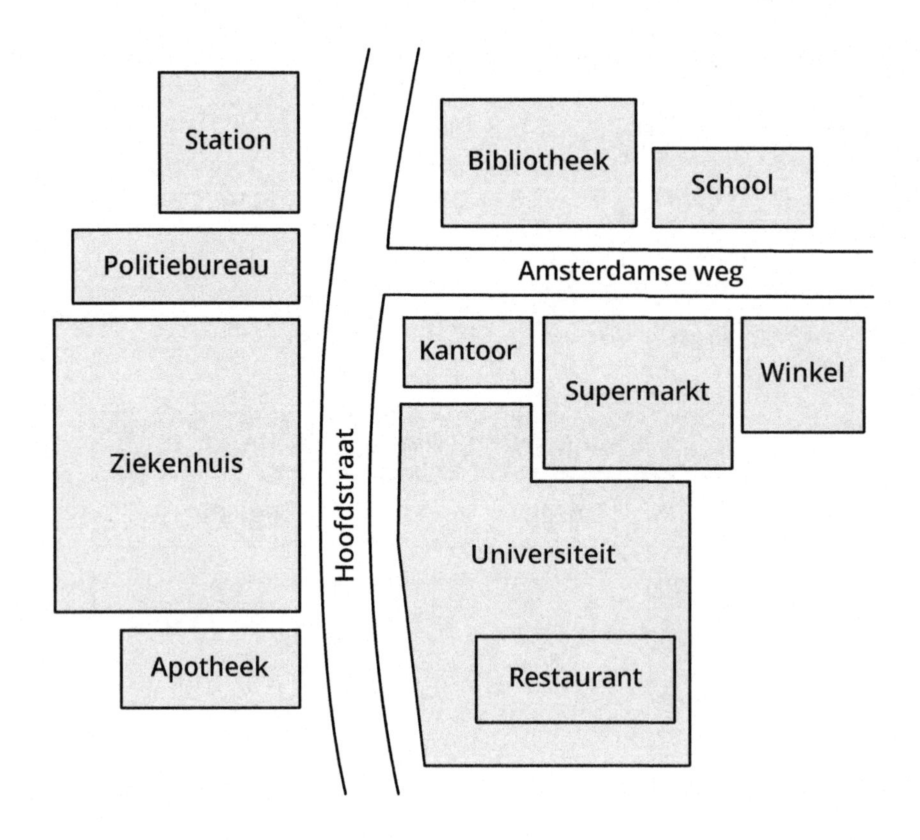

1) Follow the instructions given and say which place it takes you to. The first one has been filled out as an example.

1) U bent in de apotheek. Sla links af in de Hoofdstraat, loop langs het ziekenhuis.Op de hoek van de Amsterdamse weg, tegenover het kantoor __**is de bibliotheek**__.

2) U staat voor de school. Sla rechts af en loop langs de bibliotheek tot de hoek met de Amsterdamse weg. Sla links af en loop langs het kantoor. U bent op de Hoofdstraat. Aan de linkerkant is ______________________________.

3) Je staat voor het station. Sla rechts af. Loop langs het politiebureau. Aan de rechterkant van de Hoofdstraat, naast de apotheek is ______________________________.

4) Je staat voor de universiteit. Sla rechts af en loop langs de Hoofdstraat tot aan de bibliotheek. Naast de supermarkt, tegenover de bibliotheek is ______________________________.

2) Change these affirmative sentences into questions. Follow the example below:

1) De bus is bij de bushalte. → Question: *Is de bus bij de bushalte?*

2) Jij heet Armando.

____.

3) De toeristen lopen op het plein.

____.

4) Zij neemt de bus.

____.

5) Jullie zijn in de apotheek.

____.

6) Zij hebben een schoenenwinkel.

____.

7) De kinderen fietsen naar school.

____.

8) Je zoekt het restaurant.

____.

3) Choose the correct question word from the three options given. Make sure to read the answer to the question for the context you need. The first one has been filled out as an example

1) (Wie/Wat/**Waar**) is het restaurant? - In de universiteit.

2) (Hoeveel/Wanneer/Hoe) kost het ticket? - 26 euro.

3) (Hoe/Wat/Welk) station is dit? - Dit is Station Amsterdam Amstel.

4) (Waar/Wat/Hoeveel) is uw naam? - Mijn naam is Erik van den Bogaarden.

5) (Wie/Hoe/Wanneer) is de dokter hier? - De dokter is Dr. John Terhorst.

6) (Wie/Wanneer/Waar) is de haven? - Tegenover het vliegveld.

7) (Wanneer/Hoe/Wat) gaat de winkel open? - Om 9 uur 's ochtends.

4) Write the correct plural of the noun given. The first one has been filled out as an example.

1) Brief ____**brieven**____.

2) Apotheek ________.

3) Ziekenhuis ________.

4) Chef ________.

5) Beroep ________.

6) Tram ________.

7) Restaurant ________.

8) Vliegveld ________.

9) Auto ________.

10) School ________.

5) Complete the sentences with *er is* (there is) or *er zijn* (there are). All the examples are affirmative. The first one has been filled out as an example.

1) ____**Er zijn**____ motors.

2) ________ een huis.

3) ________ 30 winkels.

4) ________ boeken.

5) ________ twee stations.

6) ________ meisjes.

7) ________ een haven.

8) ________ drie verpleegsters.

6) Rewrite the sentences from exercise 5 with *er is* (there is) or *er zijn* (there are) to make them into questions. The first one has been filled out as an example.

1) ____**Zijn er**____ motors?

2) ________ een huis?

3) ________ 30 winkels?

4) ________ boeken?

5) ________ twee stations?

6) ________ meisjes?

7) ________ een haven?

8) ________ drie verpleegsters?

3.4 WOORDENLIJST
VOCABULARY LIST

(de) apotheek	pharmacy
(de) auto	car
(de) bibliotheek	library
(de) bus	bus
(de) fiets	bicycle, bike
(de) haven	port
(de) hoek	corner
(de) motor	motorcycle, engine
(de) naam	name
(de) school	school
(de) sporthal	sports hall
(de) stad	city
(de) supermarkt	supermarket
(de) taxi	taxi
(de) tram	tram
(de) universiteit	university
(de) voetganger	pedestrian
(de) vrachtauto / vrachtwagen	truck
(de) weg	road
(de) winkel	shop
(het) blad	leaf
(het) plein	square
(het) kantoor	office
(het) openbaar vervoer	public transport
(het) politiebureau	police station
(het) restaurant	restaurant
(het) station	railway station
(het) vliegveld	airport
(het) zwembad	swimming pool

aan de linkerkant	on the left-hand side
aan de rechterkant	on the right-hand side
achter	behind
bedankt	thanks
daar	there
dichtbij	close to, nearby
er is	there is
er zijn	there are
fietsen	to cycle
fijne dag	(have a) nice day
gids	tour guide
hartelijk bedankt	thank you very much
hier	here
hoeveel	how much/many
in	in(side)
langs	past
links	left
lopen	to walk
maar	but
meervoud	plural
misschien	maybe
naast	next to
nemen	to take
niet	not
onder	under
op	on
rechtdoor	straight ahead
rechts	right
sla af	turn
sla links af	turn left
sla rechts af	turn right
tegenover	opposite

tot, totaan	until
ver	far
verdwaald	lost
vol	full
voor	for
waarom	why
wanneer	when
wat	what
welk(e)	which
wie	who
zelfstandig naamwoord	noun
zitten	to sit, to be located
zoeken	to look for

Boodschappen doen

Doing the groceries

4
Deel
Unit

Unit 4 focuses on teaching you the vocabulary of staple foods, basic phrases you need to buy groceries, numbers from 11 to 1000, as well as adjectives to describe food, and basic linking words. You'll also learn how to manage negation in Dutch, learn the demonstrative pronouns and learn more about word order.

VOCABULARY	GRAMMAR
- Staple foods - Numbers 11-1000 - Adjectives to describe food - Linking words	- Negation in Dutch - Demonstrative pronouns - Word order

TRACK 18 Below is a list of staple foods. Listen to the audio and read along to learn these food items and their correct pronunciation.

ALLEDAAGSE ETENSWAREN (STAPLE FOODS)					
Groenten (Vegetables)			Fruit (Fruit)		Overig (Others)
(de) doperwten	(de) uien	(de) sla	(de) appels	(de) bananen	(het) brood
(de) spinazie	(de) tomaten	(de) aardappelen	(de) peren	(de) druiven	(het) vlees
(de) knoflook	(de) bloemkool	(de) rode bieten	(de) aardbeien	(de) meloen	(de) vis
(de) kidneybonen	(de) witte kool	(de) komkommer	(de) kersen	(de) mandarijnen	(de) kaas
(de) bleekselderij	(de) wortels	(de) asperges	(de) sinaasappels	(de) perziken	(de) melk

4.1 DUTCH IN CONTEXT: EVEN BOODSCHAPPEN DOEN

GETTING SOME QUICK GROCERIES

TRACK 19 Paulien is going to the supermarket with her mother Janine. Listen to their conversation and read along.

Paulien: *Mama, heb je de boodschappenlijst?*

Janine: *Ja hoor. Er staat: 3 kilo aardappelen, 1 kilo wortels, 4 tomaten, 1 komkommer, 2 kilo appels, een halve kilo kersen, 2 liter melk, 1 brood en een halve kilo kaas.*

Paulien: *Goed. We hebben de groenten al. Nu nog het fruit, de kaas en de melk.*

Janine: *Ja, dat klopt.*

Paulien: *Mama, maar ik wil ook deze aardbeien kopen. Ze kosten €19,50 per kilo.*

Janine: *O, dat is te duur!*

Paulien: *Maar ik vind aardbeien heel lekker!*

Janine: *Dat begrijp ik, maar ze zijn te duur. Helaas pindakaas. Kom, we hebben nu alles. Laten we gaan betalen.*

Paulien: *Oké dan...*

Useful phrases from the conversation:

Ja hoor. → Sure.

Een halve kilo kaas. → Half a kilo of cheese.

Ja, dat klopt. → Yes, that's right.

Oh, dat is te duur. → Oh, that's too expensive.

Maar ik vind aardbeien heel lekker. → But I really like strawberries.

Helaas pindakaas. → Too bad.

Laten we gaan betalen. → Let's go pay.

Oké dan. → Alright then.

WERKWOORDEN VOOR BOODSCHAPPEN DOEN (VERBS FOR GROCERY SHOPPING)	
Dutch	**English**
kopen	to buy
verkopen	to sell
kosten	to cost
bestellen	to order
betalen	to pay
willen	to want
staan	to stand / be located
houden van	to like/love something
lekker vinden	to like (for food)

VOEGWOORDEN (LINKING WORDS)	
Dutch	**English**
en	and
maar	but
of	or
daarom	that's why

INTERESSANTE WEETJES

Helaas pindakaas loosely translates to "too bad, peanut butter". There's no real relationship with peanut butter, except that the two words rhyme. Use this Dutch expression and you'll sound more like a native!

DUTCH IN CONTEXT: WAT VIND JIJ LEKKER? WHAT DO YOU LIKE?

TRACK 20 Gerdien and Roland are discussing what foods they do and don't like. Have a look at the vocabulary box below for the meaning of the adjectives they use. Listen to the conversations and read along.

Gerdien: *Roland, vind jij olijven lekker?*

Roland: *Nee, helemaal niet! Die vind ik veel te zout. Jij wel?*

Gerdien: *Ja, ik vind ze heerlijk! En hou je van vis?*

Roland: *Ik ben dol op vis! Vooral zalm, maar helaas is dat niet goedkoop.*

Gerdien: *Dat klopt. Ik hou niet van vis, maar ik ben niet vegetarisch. Ik vind het gewoon niet lekker.*

Roland: *Ik begrijp het. Hou je van Indonesisch eten?*

Gerdien: *Ja, dat vind ik ook heerlijk! Ik hou van pittige recepten. Jij ook?*

Roland: *Ja! Wil je dit weekend met mij uit eten bij het nieuwe Indonesische restaurant?*

Gerdien: *Leuk! Afgesproken.*

Useful phrases from the conversation:

Questions:

Vind jij olijven lekker? → Do you like olives?

Jij wel? → Do you? (Used after the speaker has just made a negative statement)

En hou je van vis? → And do you like fish?

Hou je van Indonesisch eten? → Do you like Indonesian food?

Jij ook? → You too?

Wil je met mij uit eten? → Do you want to go out for dinner with me?

Answers:

Nee, helemaal niet! → No, not at all!

Die vind ik veel te zout. → I think they're way too salty.

Ik ben dol op vis! → I love fish!

Vooral zalm, maar helaas is dat niet goedkoop. → Especially salmon, but unfortunately it's not cheap!

Ik vind het gewoon niet lekker. → I just don't like it.

Leuk! Afgesproken. → Great! It's a deal/date.

BIJVOEGLIJK NAAMWOORD OM ETEN TE BESCHRIJVEN (ADJECTIVES TO DESCRIBE FOODS)

Dutch	English
lekker	tasty
heerlijk	delicious
vies	disgusting
zoet	sweet
zout	salty
hartig	savory
pittig	spicy
mild	mild
duur	expensive
goedkoop	cheap

INTERESSANTE WEETJES

Staple foods of the typical Dutch diet are bread, cheese and other dairy products, and potatoes. If you go to the Netherlands, make sure to try *boerenkool*, a type of mashed potato mixed with boiled kale leaves, served with a large, juicy sausage.

VOCABULARY: NUMMERS 11-1000 NUMBERS 11-1000

In order to say all the prices when going shopping, we need to know more numbers than just 0-10! We've split the numbers up into groups to make sure not to overwhelm you. We'll start with numbers 11-30 which are listed in the table below.

NUMMERS 11-30 (NUMBERS 11-30)	
11. elf	21. eenentwintig*
12. twaalf	22. tweeëntwintig
13. dertien	23. drieëntwintig
14. veertien	24. vierentwintig
15. vijftien	25. vijfentwintig
16. zestien	26. zesentwintig
17. zeventien	27. zevenentwintig
18. achttien	28. achtentwintig
19. negentien	29. negenentwintig
20. twintig	30. dertig

NUMMERS 31-2000 (NUMBERS 31-2000)	
31. eenendertig	100. honderd
32. tweeëndertig	200. tweehonderd
33. drieëndertig (etc)	300. driehonderd
40. veertig	400. vierhonderd
50. vijftig	500. vijfhonderd
60. zestig	600. zeshonderd
70. zeventig	700. zevenhonderd
80. tachtig	800. achthonderd
90. negentig	900. negenhonderd
	1000. duizend
	2000. tweeduizend

* Please note that, unlike in English, in numbers from twenty onward, the ones come before the tens. When translated literally it says: one-and-twenty. The second or third e gets a diaeresis for the correct pronunciation. *Een* in *eenentwintig* doesn't get an accent (*één*) which it sometimes gets when it is emphasized in the sentence but the pronunciation is the same.

For the really large numbers, follow the table below. Be aware that it is a bit confusing: a billion in English is a *miljard* in Dutch and a *biljoen* in Dutch is a trillion in English. When investing, a mistake in the name of such numbers can cost you dearly!

NUMBER	DUTCH	ENGLISH
1,000,000	*miljoen*	million
1,000,000,000	*miljard*	billion
1,000,000,000	*biljoen*	trillion

4.2 GRAMMAR: AANWIJZENDE VOORNAAMWOORDEN

DEMONSTRATIVE PRONOUNS

Let's learn the demonstrative pronouns, which are especially useful when you go grocery shopping, in case you need to point out exactly which item you want to buy. There are four demonstrative pronouns:

SINGULAR	CLOSE TO THE SPEAKER (THIS)	FAR AWAY FROM THE SPEAKER (THAT)
de-words	*deze*	*die*
het-words	*dit*	*dat*

Deze/die and *dit/dat* are the words for this/that. *Deze* en *die* are used for words with the article *de*. *Dit* en *dat* are used for words with the article *het*.

PLURAL	CLOSE TO THE SPEAKER (THIS)	FAR AWAY FROM THE SPEAKER (THAT)
de-words	deze	die

As all plural words have the article *de* the same words *deze* and *die* as in single words are used. Here are some examples:

	CLOSE TO THE SPEAKER	FAR AWAY FROM THE SPEAKER
de auto	*deze auto*	*die auto*
de auto's	*deze auto's*	*die auto's*
het huis	*dit huis*	*dat huis*
de huizen	*deze huizen*	*die huizen*

You usually use these demonstrative words *deze, die, dit, dat* directly in front of nouns:

Deze pen en dit boek zijn van mij. → This pen and this book are mine.

Die gum en dat potlood zijn van jou. → That eraser and that pencil are yours.

Deze tafels en die stoelen staan in het klaslokaal. → These tables and those chairs are in the class room.

But when it is clear what you are talking about, you can also leave the noun out and use the demonstratives on their own. In English, you would often add one:

Is dat jouw pen of deze? → Is that your pen or this one?

Wil je deze trui of die daar? → Do you want this sweater or that one over there?

GRAMMAR: ONTKENNENDE ZINNEN NEGATIVE SENTENCES

Changing affirmative sentences into negative sentences in Dutch is a little more complicated than forming questions, which is why we're treating negation separately. Let's delve into the ins and outs. In a nutshell, there are two words, *niet* and *geen*, that roughly take the meaning of not and no (when followed by an object). Below is the explanation oft when to use each one.

Niet

The most common way to make negative sentences is *niet*, which translates to "not" in most cases. Examples:

a. *Ik betaal die tomaten* ***niet***. (I'm not paying for those tomatoes.)

b. *Die auto is* ***niet*** *snel*. (That car isn't fast.)

c. *Zij wonen* ***niet*** *in Nederland*. (They don't live in the Netherlands.)

Unlike in English, the position of *niet* within the sentence varies. It often comes at the end of the sentence, as illustrated by example a. But it will precede adjectives and prepositions, as illustrated by examples b and c.

Geen

We mostly use the word ***geen*** when replacing indefinite articles. Examples:

- **a.** *Hier zijn* ***geen*** *winkels*. (There are no stores here.)
- **b.** *Ik spreek* ***geen*** *Russisch*. (I don't speak Russian.)
- **c.** *Hij drinkt* ***geen*** *koffie*. (He doesn't drink coffee.)

Example b illustrates the rule that whenever the negation is about a language, we use *geen*. Example c illustrates the rule that whenever the negation is about an uncountable object such as water, beer, coffee, etc, we use *geen*.

Here are some more examples of affirmative sentences and their negative counterpart:

Niet

Hij verkoopt zijn huis. → *Hij verkoopt zijn huis* ***niet***.

De arts woont in de stad. → *De arts woont* ***niet*** *in de stad.*

U houdt van vis. → *U houdt* ***niet*** *van vis.*

Het meisje is aardig. → *Het meisje is* ***niet*** *aardig.*

Geen

Ik heb een idee. → *Ik heb* ***geen*** *idee.*

Janine koopt appels. → *Janine koopt* ***geen*** *appels.*

Sofia spreekt Spaans. → *Sofia spreekt* ***geen*** *Spaans.*

Er zit melk in de fles. → *Er zit* ***geen*** *melk in de fles.*

GRAMMAR: WOORDVOLGORDE WORD ORDER

Whereas there are many similarities between English and Dutch, word order is one of the things where there are a few significant differences. You'll learn more about this as you learn more verb tenses, but here are some basic rules that are important to start applying right from the start.

The main verb must always be the second word in the sentence. Here are two examples where we've numbered the parts of the sentence, the functions of which will be clarified below:

1 (SUBJECT)	2 (VERB)	3 (TIME)	4 (OBJECT OR MANNER)	5 (PLACE OR OBJECT)
De schoonmaakster	**neemt**	morgen	de bus	naar haar werk.
De lerares	**stuurt**	na de les	een email	aan haar leerlingen.
We	**gaan**	later	met de auto	naar het strand.
Ik	**koop**	nooit	kaas	op de markt.
De mensen	**fietsen**	vaak	snel	door de regen.

It's important to note the order of parts 1 to 3 of the sentence. If these are included in a sentence, they will almost always follow this order unless you start the sentence with the third component (time), as will be illustrated below.

However, it is possible to bring forward part 3, as long as the rest of the parts of the sentence remain in the same order. This is shown in the table below:

3 (TIME)	2 (VERB)	1 (SUBJECT)	4 (OBJECT OR MANNER)	5 (PLACE OR OBJECT)
Morgen	**neemt**	de schoonmaakster	de bus	naar haar werk.
Na de les	**stuurt**	de lerares	een email	aan haar leerlingen.
Later	**gaan**	we	met de auto	naar het strand.
Nooit	**koop**	ik	kaas	op de markt.
Vaak	**fietsen**	de mensen	snel	door de regen.

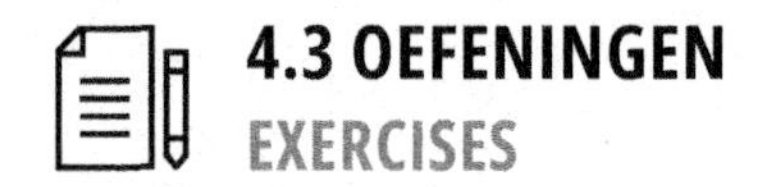

4.3 OEFENINGEN
EXERCISES

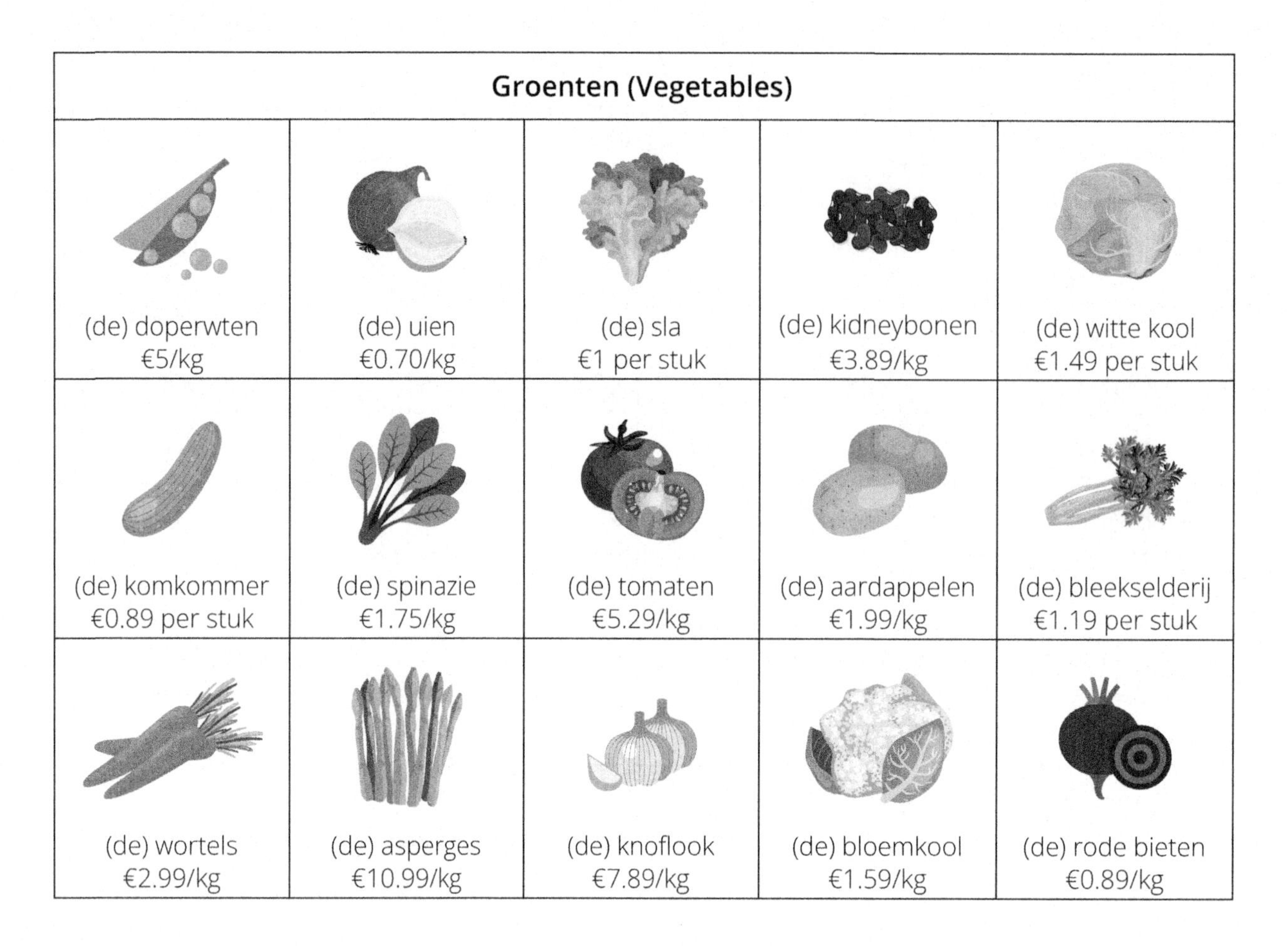

Groenten (Vegetables)				
(de) doperwten €5/kg	(de) uien €0.70/kg	(de) sla €1 per stuk	(de) kidneybonen €3.89/kg	(de) witte kool €1.49 per stuk
(de) komkommer €0.89 per stuk	(de) spinazie €1.75/kg	(de) tomaten €5.29/kg	(de) aardappelen €1.99/kg	(de) bleekselderij €1.19 per stuk
(de) wortels €2.99/kg	(de) asperges €10.99/kg	(de) knoflook €7.89/kg	(de) bloemkool €1.59/kg	(de) rode bieten €0.89/kg

1) Complete the sentences below with the correct vegetable names and prices as shown in the table above. When you finish, listen to the tape to check your answers and repeat the pronunciation of the numbers. The first one has been filled out as an example.

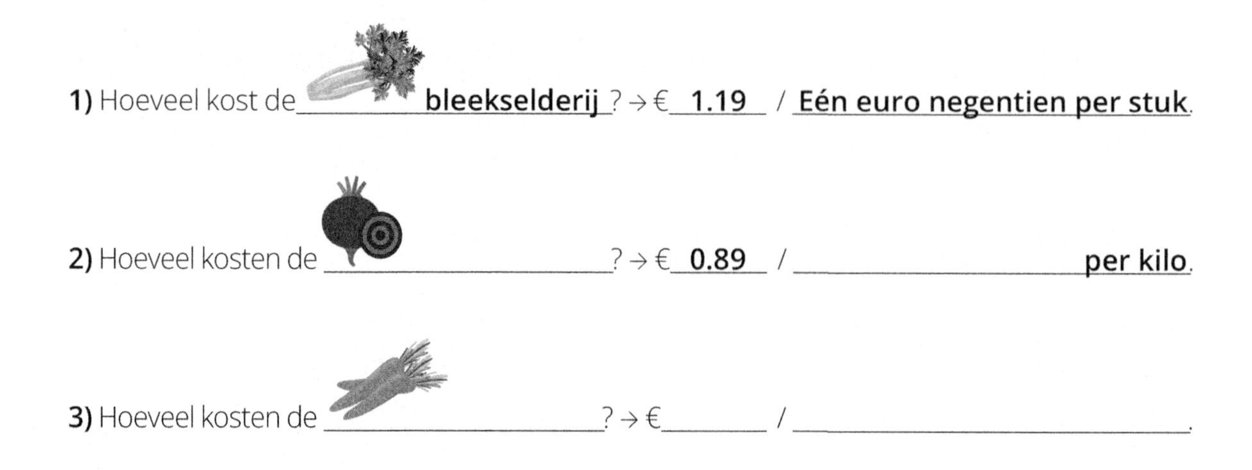

1) Hoeveel kost de **bleekselderij** ? → € **1.19** / **Eén euro negentien per stuk**.

2) Hoeveel kosten de ______ ? → € **0.89** / ______ **per kilo**.

3) Hoeveel kosten de ______ ? → €______ / ______.

4) Hoeveel kosten de ______________________? → €________ / ______________________________.

5) Hoeveel kost de ______________________? → €________ / ______________________________.

6) Hoeveel kost de ______________________? → €________ / ______________________________.

2) Write the numbers below in full. The first one has been filled out as an example.

79	**negenenzeventig**
93	______________________________.
38	______________________________.
44	______________________________.
214	______________________________.
167	______________________________.
555	______________________________.
771	______________________________.
1234	______________________________.
3411	______________________________.
6856	______________________________.
2018	______________________________.

3) Complete with the correct demonstrative pronouns: *deze, dit* or *dat.* The first one has been filled out as an example

1) Hoe heet ___**die**___ hond? (What is the name of **that** dog?)

2) Hoeveel kost ___________ brood? (How much does **this** bread cost?)

3) Hoe loop ik naar ___________ straat? (How do I walk to **that** street?)

4) Zijn ___________ sleutels van jou? (Are **these** keys yours?)

5) Waar liggen ___________ blauwe handdoeken? (Where are **those** blue towels?)

6) Ik vind ___________ ketting mooier dan die. (I like **this** necklace better than that one.)

7) ___________ auto's rijden erg hard. (**Those** cars drive very fast.)

8) Ik vind ___________ muziek heel mooi. (I like **this** music very much.)

4) Change these affirmative sentences into negative sentences, using *niet* or *geen.* The first one has been filled out as an example

1) Er zijn sinaasappels. → Er zijn **geen** sinaasappels.

2) We verkopen computers.

____.

3) De kinderen willen schoonmaken.

____.

4) Georgina houdt van kersen.

____.

5) De auto's staan goed geparkeerd.

____.

6) Mijn vrienden spreken Engels.

____.

7) De druiven zijn duur.

____.

8) Er is een supermarkt.

____.

5) Use the given sentence parts and reorder them to form a correct affirmative sentence.
The first one has been filled out as an example.

1) straks / koop / op de markt / ik / aardappelen

Ik koop straks aardappelen op de markt.

2) lopen / naar huis / snel / we / vanavond

____.

3) meteen / om 4 uur / willen / naar het vliegveld / jullie

____.

4) altijd / naar buiten / de dieren / rennen / snel

____.

5) op de markt / de student / morgen / goedkoop fruit / koopt

____.

6) iedere dag / in het ziekenhuis / die dokters en verpleegsters / werken

____.

4.4 WOORDENLIJST
VOCABULARY LIST

(de) aardappel	potato
(de) aardbei	strawberry
(de) appel	apple
(de) asperge	asparagus
(de) banaan	banana
(de) bloemkool	cauliflower
(de) boodschappen	groceries
(de) boodschappenlijst	shopping list
(de) doperwt	pea
(de) druif	grape
(de) groenten	vegetables
(de) handdoek	towel
(de) hond	dog
(de) kaas	cheese
(de) kers	cherry
(de) ketting	necklace
(de) kilo	kilo
(de) knoflook	garlic
(de) komkommer	cucumber
(de) mandarijn	tangerine
(de) markt	market
(de) melk	milk
(de) meloen	melon
(de/het) mens	person, human being
(de) muziek	music
(de) peer	pear
(de) perzik	peach
(de) pindakaas	peanut butter
(de) regen	rain

(de) rode bieten	beets
(de) selderij	celery
(de) sinaasappel	orange
(de) sla	lettuce
(de) sleutel	key
(de) sperziebonen	green beans
(de) spinazie	spinach
(de) stad	city
(de) ui	onion
(de) vis	fish
(de) winkel	store
(de) witte kool	white cabbage
(de) wortel	carrot, root
(het) brood	bread
(het) strand	beach
(het) vlees	meat
(het) werk	work
achtentwintig	twenty-eight
achthonderd	eight hundred
achttien	eighteen
afgesproken	agreed
al	already
alles	everything
begrijpen	to understand
bestellen	to order
betalen	to pay
biljoen	trillion
daarom	therefore
dat	that
dertien	thirteen
dertig	thirty
deze	this, these

die	that, those
dit	this
drieëndertig	thirty-three
drieëntwintig	twenty-three
driehonderd	three hundred
duizend	thousand
eenendertig	thirty-one
eenentwintig	twenty-one
elf	eleven
en	and
geen	no
goedkoop	cheap
half	half
hartig	savory
heerlijk	delicious
helaas	unfortunately
helemaal niet	not at all
honderd	hundred
houden van	to love
ieder	each, every
kloppen	to be correct, to knock
kopen	to buy
kosten	to cost
lekker	tasty
lekker vinden	to like (food)
meteen	right away
miljard	billion
miljoen	million
morgen	tomorrow
negenentwintig	twenty-nine
negenhonderd	nine hundred
negentien	nineteen

negentig	ninety
nemen	to take
nog	still
nooit	never
of	or
ook	also
parkeren	to park
per stuk	per unit
pittig	spicy
rennen	to run
rijden	to drive
schoonmaken	to clean
snel	fast
spreken	to speak
staan	to stand
tachtig	eighty
twaalf	twelve
tweeduizend	two thousand
tweeëndertig	thirty-two
tweeëntwintig	twenty-two
tweehonderd	two hundred
twintig	twenty
vaak	often
veertien	fourteen
veertig	forty
verkopen	to sell
vierentwintig	twenty-four
vierhonderd	four hundred
vies	dirty
vijfentwintig	twenty-five
vijfhonderd	five hundred
vijftien	fifteen

vijftig	fifty
vooral	mainly
zesentwintig	twenty-six
zeshonderd	six hundred
zestien	sixteen
zestig	sixty
zevenentwintig	twenty-seven
zevenhonderd	seven hundred
zeventien	seventeen
zeventig	seventy
zoet	sweet
zout	salt

Mijn routine
My routine

5
Deel
Unit

Unit 5 focuses on teaching you the days of the week and months of the year, how to describe the weather, and several useful expressions to talk about time. You'll also learn the direct and indirect object pronouns, how to tell the time and how to conjugate adjectives.

VOCABULARY	GRAMMAR
- Days of the week and months	- Telling the time
- Time expressions	- Direct and indirect object pronouns
- Describing the weather	- Conjugation of adjectives

5.1 DUTCH IN CONTEXT: MIJN WEKELIJKSE ROUTINE

MY WEEKLY ROUTINE

TRACK 21 The table below shows Marijke's weekly schedule. She's a part-time physiotherapist in the Dutch city of Groningen. Have a look at her schedule and read along as you listen to her talk to a friend about her activities.

	MAANDAG	DINSDAG	WOENSDAG	DONDERDAG	VRIJDAG	ZATERDAG	ZONDAG
's ochtends	8-12: werk		8-12: werk	schoonmaken	8-12: werk	fietsen	
's middags	naar de markt	1-6: werk		1-6: werk			ouders bezoeken
's avonds			dansles				

Klaas: *Hoi Marijke, wat doe je meestal op maandag?*

Marijke: *Ik werk 's ochtends van 8 tot 12 en 's middags ga ik naar de markt.*

Klaas: *Werk je iedere ochtend?*

Marijke: *Nee. Op maandag, woensdag en vrijdag werk ik 's ochtends en op dinsdag en donderdag 's middags.*

Klaas: *En wanneer bezoek je je ouders?*

Marijke: *Ik bezoek mijn ouders op zondagmiddag.*

Klaas: *Wat doe je op zaterdag?*

Marijke: *Ik ga vaak met mijn man fietsen op zaterdag.*

Useful phrases from the conversation:

Wat doe je meestal op maandag? → What do you usually do on Mondays?

Werk je iedere ochtend? → Do you work every morning?

Ik werk 's ochtends van 8 tot 12. → I work from 8 to 12 in the morning.

En wanneer bezoek je je ouders? → And when do you visit your parents?

Wat doe je op zaterdag? → What do you do on Saturdays?

More time expressions

Let's take a closer look at how to refer to times of day in Dutch.

These are the parts of the day:

De ochtend, de morgen → The morning

De middag → The afternoon

De avond → The evening

De nacht → The night

But if you want to refer to an activity that happens during one of those parts of the day, you have to place 's before the word and add an s at the end.

's ochtends, 's morgens → in the morning

's middags → in the afternoon

's avonds → in the evening

's nachts → at night

TIJDSAANDUIDINGEN (TIME EXPRESSIONS)	
Dutch	**English**
(de) ochtend	morning
(de) middag	afternoon
(de) avond	evening
(de) nacht	night
(de) dag	day
(de) minuut	minute
(het) uur	hour
(de) week	week
vandaag	today
morgen	tomorrow
ieder(e)	every
soms	sometimes
vaak	often
meestal	usually
altijd	always
nooit	never

We also use the above when we want to clarify whether we're referring to eight o'clock in the morning or evening. Example: Het is acht uur 's avonds (it's eight o'clock at night).

If you want to combine the day of the week with the part of the day, you attach the part of the day directly to the name of the day.

maandagavond → Monday evening

vrijdagnacht → Friday night

woensdagochtend → Wednesday morning

zondagmiddag → Sunday afternoon

Lastly, if you want to refer to the morning/afternoon/evening/night of the same day, you would add van to the word. Depending on if that part of the day is before or after the time of speaking, it would refer to the past or future.

vanochtend, vanmorgen → this morning

vanmiddag → this afternoon

vanavond → this evening

vannacht → tonight/last night (this will depend on context)

Also, don't forget that the days in Dutch should not be capitalized.

🛈 INTERESSANTE WEETJES

Timekeeping is serious business in the Netherlands, especially for work appointments. Birthday party invitations usually mention the time the party is due to start — and even what time it is planned to end!

DUTCH IN CONTEXT: HOE WORDT HET WEER VANDAAG?

WHAT WILL THE WEATHER BE LIKE TODAY?

Look at the weather vocabulary in the tables below.

Het is heet (It's hot)	*Het is koud* (It's cold)	*Het is zonnig (*It's sunny)	*Het waait* (It's windy)
Het is bewolkt (It's cloudy)	*Gedeeltelijk bewolkt* (Partly cloudy)	*Het regent* (It's raining)	*Het is mistig* (It's foggy)
Het sneeuwt (It's snowing)	*Het onweert* (There's a thunderstorm)	*Bliksem* (Lightning)	*Er is een regenboog* (There's a rainbow)

WOORDENLIJST VOOR HET WEER (WEATHER VOCABULARY)	
Dutch	**English**
Het is lekker weer	The weather is nice
Het is mooi weer	The weather is beautiful
Het is slecht weer	The weather is bad.
Hoeveel graden is het vandaag?	How many degrees is it today?
Het is 20 graden	It's 20 degrees
Het vriest	It's below freezing
koel	cool
mild	mild
heet	hot
wisselvallig	changeable (weather)
(de) temperatuur	temperature
(de) regen	rain
(de) sneeuw	snow
(de) wolk	cloud
(het) ijs	ice
(de) hittegolf	heat wave
(de) lente, (het) voorjaar	spring
(de) zomer	summer
(de) herfst, (het) najaar	fall
(de) winter	winter
(het) seizoen	season
graden	degrees

MAANDEN VAN HET JAAR (MONTHS OF THE YEAR)	
Dutch	**English**
januari	January
februari	February
maart	March
april	April
mei	May
juni	June
juli	July
augustus	August
september	September
oktober	October
november	November
december	December

TRACK 22 The text below contains a description of the climate in the Netherlands in a typical year. Listen and read along.

De winter (december-februari)

Tijdens de wintermaanden is het erg koud in Nederland. Het is gemiddeld tussen 0 en 7 graden Celsius. Het vriest veel, soms meerdere dagen achter elkaar. Sommige kanalen en meren bevriezen in deze maanden. Het sneeuwt ook vaak en dan valt er tussen de 2 en 20 cm sneeuw.

De lente (maart-mei)

Vanaf maart stijgt de temperatuur snel. In maart is de hoogste temperatuur overdag gemiddeld 10,5 graden, maar in mei is dat al 18,3 graden. Van maart tot mei regent het weinig. Het regent meer in de zomer en de herfst. Het gezegde: "April doet wat 'ie wil," geeft aan dat april erg veranderlijk is. Het ene jaar is het nog koud in april, het andere lijkt het al zomer.

De zomer (juni-augustus)

Veel buitenlanders verbazen zich over hoe warm het in Nederland is in de zomer. De gemiddeld hoogste temperatuur tussen juni en augustus ligt tussen de 20,9 en 23,1 graden. Als er een hittegolf is, kan de temperatuur soms tot 35 graden oplopen! Het regent ook het meest tijdens deze maanden.

De herfst (september-november)

In de herfst valt er nog veel regen. De temperatuur daalt snel tijdens deze maanden. In september is de gemiddeld hoogste temperatuur nog 19,5 graden, maar in november is dat maar 9,9. Het aantal uren zon verandert veel in het najaar. Hoewel er in september nog rond de 152 uren zon zijn, is dat in november maar rond de 67 uren.

Useful phrases from the text:

Tijdens de wintermaanden is het erg koud. → It's very cold during the winter months.

Het vriest veel, soms meerdere dagen achter elkaar. → The temperature is often below freezing, sometimes several days in a row.

Het sneeuwt ook vaak. → It frequently snows too.

Van maart tot mei regent het juist weinig. → From March to May it actually doesn't rain much.

April doet wat 'ie wil. → April does what it wants.

Als er een hittegolf is, kan de temperatuur soms tot 35 graden oplopen. → When there's a heat wave, the temperature can go up as high as 35 degrees.

Het aantal zonuren verandert veel in het najaar. → The number of hours of sunshine changes a lot during fall.

5.2 GRAMMAR: KLOKKIJKEN

TELLING THE TIME

We use the 12-hour clock in everyday speech. The 24-hour clock is used only in written timetables and programs, etc. To tell the time in Dutch, we divide the clock in half: the top centers around the full hour and the bottom centers around the half hour. This is different from the way we tell the time in English, where the 2 halves are positioned vertically. This is illustrated by the image on the right:

Expressing the time in the top half of the Dutch clock works the same as with the English clock. The word voor is used to say 'to' and over to say 'past'. Een kwart is short for een kwartier, meaning a quarter of an hour or 15 minutes.

Here are some examples to help you understand this:

2.45: *kwart voor drie* → a quarter to three

3.50: *tien voor vier* → ten to four

5.05: *vijf over vijf* → five past five

5.00: *vijf uur* → five o'clock

There are several things to take into account when expressing the time in the bottom half of the Dutch clock. The biggest (and most confusing) difference with English is the way "half past" the hour is used.

Look at the following examples:

12.30: *half één* → half past twelve

4.30: *half vijf* → half past four

8.30: *half negen* → half past eight

As you can see, in Dutch we don't refer to the hour before, but to the hour coming up!

The other difference is the way we can use voor and over in reference to the half hour rather than the full hour.

Here are some examples:

2.20: *tien voor half drie** → literally: ten to half past two

3.25: *vijf voor half vier* → literally: five to half past three

9.35: *vijf over half tien* → literally: five past half past nine

4.40: *tien over half vijf** → literally: ten past half past four

* Twenty minutes past and to the hour can also be expressed more similarly to English: Het is twintig over twee (it's twenty past two) and het is twintig voor acht (it's twenty to eight).

GRAMMAR: LIJDENDE EN MEEWERKENDE VORMEN VAN PERSOONLIJKE VOORNAAMWOORDEN DIRECT AND INDIRECT OBJECT PRONOUNS

As with the subject pronouns, most have a stressed and an unstressed version. The unstressed version is used most of the time, particularly when speaking. When you used the stressed version, there is usually a reason why you want to emphasize the pronoun:

Example with the unstressed object pronoun:

Kun je ***me*** *helpen?*
(Can you help me?)

In the following sentence, we've changed the unstressed me to mij:

Kun je ***mij*** *helpen?* → Can you help **me**?

The intonation of the second example would be different too, placing the emphasis on mij, and this sentence indicates a feeling of "I would like you to be helping me rather than helping anyone else."

The table below lists the object pronouns in Dutch.

	OBJECT PRONOUN IN ENGLISH	UNSTRESSED	STRESSED
Singular	me	*me*	*mij*
	you	*je*	*jou*
	you (formal)	*u*	*u*
	him	*('m)**	*hem*
	her	*(d'r)**	*haar*
	it	*('t)**	*het*
Plural	us	*ons*	*ons*
	you (formal)	*u*	*u*
	them	*ze*	*ze (objects only), hun, hen***

* The unstressed forms in brackets are mostly used in the spoken form, and in informal literature but usually not formal literature.

** The reason there are two object pronouns (hun and hen) for the third person plural is because this is the only case where a difference is made between direct and indirect objects.

Please note that the third person singular object pronouns hem and haar are also used to refer to objects if they use the article de. Example: Het meisje heeft de rugzak. Ze heeft hem. (The girl has the backpack. She's got it.)

Positioning of the object pronouns

Here are some examples that show that the position of the object pronoun is usually similar to that in English:

Ik versta u niet. → I can't hear you.

Ik geef hem het boek. → I give him the book.

Ik gaf haar de pen. → I gave her the pen.

Ik vind hem heel aardig. → I like him very much.

More about when to use *hun* or *hen*

When using the stressed form, we use hen as a direct object and hun as an indirect object.

Hen:

Ik zie hen. → I see them.

We brengen hen naar de stad. → We take them to the city.

Hij bedankt hen. → He thanks them.

Hoe gaat het met hen? → How are they? (Hen is also used to follow a preposition: met)

Hun:

Jij geeft hun een boek. → You give them a book.

Vraag je hun te komen? → Will you ask them to come?

Ze:

Heb je ze gezien? → Have you seen them?

Geef je ze aan haar? → Will you give them to her?

Hun and hen are only ever used to refer to people, never objects. Ze can be used to refer to plural nouns that are objects, not people.

GRAMMAR: VERVOEGING VAN BIJVOEGLIJKE NAAMWOORDEN
CONJUGATION OF ADJECTIVES

In Dutch, when we place adjectives in front of a noun, in most cases you will need to add an -e to the end of the adjective. Have a look at the following examples:

Het weer is mild. → The weather is mild.

but:

Het milde weer. → The mild weather.

De kamer is koel. → The room is cool.

but:

De koele kamer. → The cool room.

Please note that this often involves changing the spelling. If the adjective has two syllables, one must be removed for the conjugated version (groot becomes grote, and heet becomes hete). Likewise, if the adjective is a three letter-word with a short vowel sound and ends in a consonant, this last consonant must be doubled (wit becomes witte, and vol becomes volle).

Also, for adjectives that end in -s, the s changes to z after adding the e, and for adjectives that end in -f, the f changes to v.

Het meisje is lief. → The girl is sweet.

but:

Het lieve meisje. → The sweet girl.

De vis is vies. → The fish is disgusting.

but:

De vieze vis. → The disgusting fish.

Exceptions

You're probably used to this by now: every grammar rule in Dutch has a handful of exceptions too! Below there is a list of situations where it's not necessary to add an e to the adjective.

1. **If the adjective precedes a neuter singular noun without an article**

   With neuter noun, we refer to the nouns whose article is het. Examples:

   a. *slecht weer* (awful weather) *but het slechte weer*

   b. *klein huis* (small house) *but het kleine huis*

   c. *fijn seizoen* (nice season) *but het fijne seizoen*

2. **If the adjective precedes a neuter singular noun after the words *een, geen, veel, een beetje, elk, genoeg, ieder, menig, weinig, welk, zo'n, zulk***

   Examples:

   a. *geen warm water* (no hot water)

   b. *een nieuw station* (a train station)

   c. *veel vers sap* (a lot of fresh juice)

   d. *zo'n leuk jongetje* (such a cute kid)

3. **If the adjective ends in -en or -e**

   Examples:

   a. *roze, oranje* (pink, orange)

   b. *gebroken, gesloten, houten* (broken, closed, wooden)

   c. *gouden, zilveren, open* (gold, silver, open)

4. **If the adjective belongs to a group of adjectives borrowed from another language, they don't take an e**

   Examples:

   a. *kaki* (khaki-colored)

   b. *indigo* (indigo-colored)

   c. *super* (super)

5. **If the adjective belongs to a group of fixed adjective-noun combination**

   There isn't a rule which defines what is considered a "fixed combination", you will have to pay attention when you see these to learn them one by one.

   Examples:

   a. *het openbaar vervoer* (public transport)

   b. *het hoger onderwijs* (higher education)

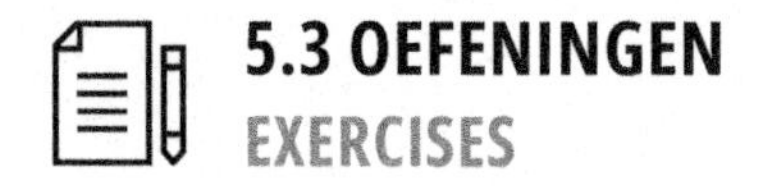

5.3 OEFENINGEN
EXERCISES

1) Look at the times and write the time next to it, in full. The first one has been filled out as an example.

1) 08:10 – Het is tien over acht.

2) 10:15 – ____________________.

3) 11:20 – ____________________.

4) 02:30 – ____________________.

5) 04:35 – ____________________.

6) 06:45 – ____________________.

7) 07:55 – ____________________.

8) 09:00 – ____________________.

2) Look at philosophy student Maarten's weekly schedule and complete the sentences about it. The first one has been filled out as an example.

	's ochtends	*'s middags*	*'s avonds*
maandag	9-1: universiteit	3: naar de sportschool	
dinsdag		1-5: universiteit	6-11: werk
woensdag	8-4: universiteit		schaakclub
donderdag		11-5: universiteit	6-11: werk
vrijdag	thuisstudie	11-5: universiteit	
zaterdag	thuisstudie		6-11: werk
zondag		voetballen	6-11: werk

1) Op maandag gaat Maarten om ___3___ uur naar de sportschool.

2) Op dinsdag gaat hij om 6 uur ______________________________.

3) Op woensdag gaat hij 's avonds naar de ______________________________.

4) Op donderdag is hij om 3 uur op de ______________________________.

5) Op vrijdag gaat hij om ______________________________ uur naar de universiteit.

6) Op zaterdag gaat hij 's avonds om ____________________ uur ____________________.

7) Op zondagmiddag gaat hij ______________________________.

3) Complete your own weekly schedule with at least one activity each day.

	maandag	***dinsdag***	***woensdag***
's ochtends			
's middags			
's avonds			

donderdag	***vrijdag***	***zaterdag***	***zondag***

4) Look at the weather forecast below and answer the questions. The first one has been filled out as an example.

	maandag	dinsdag	woensdag	donderdag	vrijdag	zaterdag
Max. temp.	10 °C	14 °C	18 °C	20 °C	25 °C	16°C

1) Welke dag wordt het heet? → Op vrijdag.

2) Wat wordt de maximale temperatuur op woensdag?

____.

3) Welke dag wordt het zonnig?

____.

4) Welke dag wordt het 25 graden?

____.

5) Welke dag waait het?

____.

6) Wat wordt de maximale temperatuur op zaterdag?

____.

7) Welke dag regent het?

____.

5) Choose the correct option from the subject and object pronouns given. The first one has been filled out as an example.

1) (**Ik**/Me) speel gitaar.

2) Heeft u nieuws voor (ik/mij)?

3) (Ze/Hun) fietsen naar het station.

4) (Wij/Ons) hebben een nieuwe fiets.

5) Wij helpen (hij/hem) met het probleem.

6) Brengen jullie (ze/hen) naar huis? (referring to people)

7) Is dit de goede sleutel? Ja, geef je (hem/het) aan Wim?

8) (Hij/Het) is mooi weer.

9) Wil je deze aardappelen kopen? Ja, doe (ze/hen) maar in het mandje.

6) Rewrite the sentence by replacing the underlined word with the correct object pronoun. The first one has been filled out as an example.

1) Jurre praat met **Paula**. → Jurre praat met **haar**.

2) Jullie schrijven **de brief**. ______________________.

3) Wij sturen een e-mail naar **de advocaten**. ______________________.

4) Heeft u vragen voor **Remy en mij**? ______________________.

5) Ze helpen **Meneer van Dijk**. ______________________.

6) We gaan **Greet** ophalen. ______________________.

7) **De komkommers** liggen op tafel. ______________________.

7) Choose the correct form of the adjective from the options given to complete the following sentences. The first one has been filled out as an example.

1) Haar huis is (**groot**/grote).
Correct answer: **groot** (the e doesn't have to be added when the adjective follows the noun)

2) Het is (lekker/lekkere) weer vandaag.

3) De (koel/koele) dag.

4) Mijn lerares is (lief/lieve).

5) Het is een (grijs/grijze) dag.

6) Het kind wil een (oranje/oranjee) gitaar.

7) Het is zo'n (mooi/mooie) herfst.

8) Wat zijn dit (heerlijk/heerlijke) aardappelen!

9) De (pittig/pittige) soep.

10) We hebben (houten/houtene) banken.

8) Complete the sentences with one of the adjectives from the box. It's not necessary to add an -e in this case, use them just as they appear in the box. The first one has been filled out as an example.

lekkere – dure – hete – ~~zout~~ – zoet – goedkoop – warm – mistige

1) Ik hou van ____**zout**____ eten.

2) Mijn zus eet graag in ______________________ restaurants.

3) In november zijn er veel ______________________ dagen.

4) Aruba is een heel ______________________ land. Het is er altijd zonnig.

5) Dat café heeft ______________________ koffie.

6) Wat zijn die aardbeien ______________________!

7) Dit jaar hebben we een erg ______________________ zomer.

8) 2 euro per t-shirt? Deze zijn zo ______________________!

5.4 WOORDENLIJST
VOCABULARY LIST

(de) avond	evening
(de) bliksem	lightning
(de) brief	letter
(de) gitaar	guitar
(de) graden	degrees
(de) herfst, (het) najaar	fall
(de) hittegolf	heat wave
(de) lente, (het) voorjaar	spring
(de) middag	afternoon
(de) minuut	minute
(de) nacht	night
(de) ochtend	morning
(de) regen	rain
(de) regenboog	rainbow
(de) rugzak	backpack
(de) sneeuw	snow
(de) sportschool	gym
(de) temperatuur	temperature
(de) week	week
(de) winter	winter
(de) wintermaanden	winter months
(de) wolk	cloud
(de) zomer	summer
(het) aantal	number, amount
(het) ijs	ice
(het) kwartier	quarter
(het) mandje	basket
(het) nieuws	news
(het) onweer	thunderstorm

(het) sap	juice
(het) seizoen	season
(het) uur	hour
(het) weer	weather
's avonds	in the evening
's middags	in the afternoon
's nachts	at night
's ochtends, 's morgens	in the morning
aardig	friendly
achter elkaar	in a row
altijd	always
april	April
augustus	August
bewolkt	cloudy
bezoeken	to visit
december	December
dinsdag	Tuesday
donderdag	Thursday
een beetje	a little bit
elk	each
erg	very, awful
februari	February
gebroken	broken
gedeeltelijk	partially
gemiddeld	average
gesloten	closed
geven	to give
grijs	gray
heet	hot
hoogst	highest
houden	to hold
houten	wooden

iedere	every
januari	January
juli	July
juni	June
koel	cool
leuk	fun
lief	sweet
liggen	to lie, to be located
maandag	Monday
maart	March
meerdere	multiple
meestal	usually
mei	May
menig	many
mistig	foggy
november	November
oktober	October
oplopen	increase
oranje	orange (color)
regenen	to rain
september	September
slecht	bad
sneeuwen	to snow
soms	sometimes
studeren	to study
sturen	to steer
thuis	at home
tijdens	during
tot	until
vaak	often
vanavond	this evening
vandaag	today

vanmiddag	this afternoon
vannacht	tonight/last night
vanochtend, vanmorgen	this morning
veranderen	to change
vers	fresh
voetballen	to play football
vriezen	to be below freezing
vrijdag	Friday
waaien	to blow (wind)
weinig	few
wisselvallig	changeable (weather)
woensdag	Wednesday
worden	to become
zaterdag	Saturday
zien	to see
zilveren	silver
zo'n	such a
zondag	Sunday
zonnig	sunny
zulk	such

Naar de huisarts
Seeing the doctor

6
Deel
Unit

Unit 6 focuses on teaching you the parts of the body, vocabulary you need for a doctor's appointment, and common interjections. You'll also learn how to use reflexive verbs, possessive adjectives, how to express possession by adding an s to the subject, and how to form the present continuous.

VOCABULARY	GRAMMAR
- Parts of the body - How to express physical ailments - Interjections	- Reflexive verbs - Possessive adjectives and possessions. - Present continuous

6.1 DUTCH IN CONTEXT: HET MENSELIJK LICHAAM

THE HUMAN BODY

TRACK 23 Look at the image of the human body parts below and listen to the audio to learn the pronunciation.

WOORDENLIJST GERELATEERD AAN DE GEZONDHEID (HEALTH-RELATED VOCABULARY)	
Dutch	**English**
(de) hoofdpijn	headache
(de) keelpijn	sore throat
(de) buikpijn	stomachache
(de) kiespijn	toothache
(de) rugpijn	backache
(de) spierpijn	sore muscle(s)
(de) allergie	allergy
(de) koorts	fever
(de) duizeligheid	dizziness
(de) verhoging	slight temperature
(de) klachten	symptoms
(de) huisarts	general practitioner
(de) spreekkamer	consultation room
(de) uitslag	rash, test results
(de) röntgenfoto	X-ray
(de) pijnstiller	painkiller
(de) zalf	ointment
(het) linkerbeen	left leg
(het) rechterbeen	right leg
(het) recept	prescription
zich zorgen maken	to worry
zich niet lekker voelen	to feel unwell
voorschrijven	to prescribe
erger worden	to get worse
last hebben van	to suffer from
meevallen	to not be that bad
in de gaten houden	to keep an eye on it
jeuken	to itch
ernstig	severe
erg	awful
pijnlijk	painful
besmettelijk	contagious
misselijk	nauseous
duizelig	dizzy
zwanger	pregnant
moe	tired
bezorgd	worried
gestrest	stressed
depressief	depressed

DUTCH IN CONTEXT: NAAR DE HUISARTS SEEING THE DOCTOR

TRACK 24 Ahmed isn't feeling well and goes to see his general practitioner, mevrouw Smit. Listen to their conversation and read along.

Huisarts:	*Goedemorgen meneer Aziz.*
Ahmed:	*Goedemorgen mevrouw Smit.*
Huisarts:	*Vertelt u het maar. Hoe voelt u zich?*
Ahmed:	*Slecht. Ik heb erg last van mijn linkerbeen. Gisteren ging ik met de bus naar de stad. Bij het uitstappen verzwikte ik mijn enkel. Ik kan nu bijna niet meer lopen. Het doet echt heel veel pijn.*
Huisarts:	*Oei. Ik zal even kijken. Doet het pijn als ik hierop druk?*
Ahmed:	*Au au, dat doet heel erg pijn! Heb ik misschien iets gebroken?*
Huisarts:	*Nou, ik denk het niet hoor, meneer Aziz. Kunt u uw tenen nog bewegen? Als u dat kan, valt het mee.*
Ahmed:	*Ja, mijn voet en tenen doen geen pijn.*
Huisarts:	*U heeft alleen uw enkel verzwikt, dat is vaak pijnlijk. Ik ga u een pijnstiller en zalf voorschrijven. Die kunt u vanmiddag bij onze apotheek ophalen. Als de pijn niet overgaat, kunt u volgende week een nieuwe afspraak maken met mijn assistente. Beterschap, meneer Aziz!*
Ahmed:	*Hartelijk bedankt, dokter Smit!*

Useful phrases from the conversation:

Vertelt u het maar. → Go ahead and tell me.

Hoe voelt u zich? → How are you feeling?

Ik heb erg last van mijn linkerbeen. → My left leg is hurting/bothering me a lot.

Ik kan nu bijna niet meer lopen. → I can hardly walk now.

Ik zal even kijken. → I'll have a look.

Doet het pijn als ik hier druk? → Does it hurt when I press here?

Nou, ik denk het niet hoor, meneer Aziz. → Well, I don't think so, Mr Aziz.

U heeft alleen uw enkel verzwikt, dat is vaak pijnlijk. → You've only sprained your ankle, that's often painful.

Beterschap, meneer Aziz! → Feel better soon, Mr Aziz!

LEERTIPS

Make sure to listen to the recorded conversations many times. It will really help you remember the vocabulary, the pronunciation, and the general rhythm of Dutch!

DUTCH IN CONTEXT: TUSSENWERPSELS INTERJECTIONS

TRACK 25 Ahmed just came back from the appointment with his general practitioner and tells his wife Amina about what the doctor said. Listen to their conversation and read along. Pay special attention to the interjections they use.

Ahmed: *Hoi Amina, ik ben terug.*

Amina: *Jeetje, wat snel!*

Ahmed: *Ja joh.*

Amina: *Nou, wat zei de dokter?*

Ahmed: *Ik heb mijn enkel verzwikt, dat is alles.*

Amina: *Goh, dus het is niet zo erg?*

Ahmed: *Nee joh, maar de pijnstiller die ik moet innemen is wel duur, maar liefst vijftien euro.*

Amina: *Tjonge jonge! Ik hoop dat je snel beter bent!*

Ahmed: *Ach, ik moet geduld hebben!*

TUSSENWERPSELS (INTERJECTIONS)			
Dutch	**English**	**Dutch**	**English**
bah	yuck	*hè hè*	finally!
joh	of course	*ach*	ah/oh well
goh	gosh	*oei*	oof
tjonge jonge	wow	*nou*	well
jeetje (mineetje)	gosh	*nou zeg*	geez
zo zo	well well	*oh jee*	uh oh

Useful phrases from the conversation:

Ik ben terug. → I'm back.

Jeetje, wat snel! → Gosh, that was quick!

Nou, wat zei de dokter? → Well, what did the doctor say?

Ik heb mijn enkel verzwikt, dat is alles! → I sprained my ankle, that's all.

Goh, dus het is niet zo ernstig! → Gosh, so it's not that serious?

Maar liefst vijftien euro. → No less than fifteen euros.

Ik hoop dat je snel beter bent! → I hope you get better soon!

Ach, ik moet geduld hebben! → Ah well, I have to be patient!

As you can see, several Dutch interjections are actually the same word twice. Several of the ones in the list above are also used double, like *ach ach*, en *oei oei*. The list above is in no way exhaustive, but it's a good start. Pay attention when listening to native Dutch speakers to see what interjections they use and when. The meaning can be hard to translate, but in context you can usually figure it out easily, especially if you hear them over and over.

INTERESSANTE WEETJES

Now that we're on the topic of body parts: here are some Dutch proverbs that use body parts:

- *Het geld groeit me niet op mijn rug.*
(Money doesn't grow on my back, i.e. I've worked hard for it)

- *Ik kom handen tekort.*
(I don't have enough hands, i.e. I have too much to do)

- *Zij draagt haar hart op haar tong.*
(She wears her heart on her tongue, i.e. she says everything she thinks)

- *Een dikke huid hebben.*
(To have thick skin, i.e. to be resilient)

6.2 GRAMMAR: WEDERKERIGE WERKWOORDEN

REFLEXIVE VERBS

Reflexive verbs are verbs that need an object pronoun that refers back to the subject of the verb. They exist in English too, but in Dutch there are more reflexive verbs than in English.

In the table below, we've conjugated the verb *zich herinneren* (to remember). It also shows how the reflexive pronouns are used:

WEDERKERIGE WERKWOORDEN (REFLEXIVE VERBS)		
	Dutch	**English**
Singular	Ik herinner ***me***	I remember
	Je herinnert ***je***	You remember
	U herinnert ***zich/u***	You remember (formal)
	Hij/ze herinnert ***zich***	He/she remembers
Plural	We herinneren ***ons***	We remember
	Jullie herinneren ***je***	You remember
	U herinnert ***zich,u***	You remember (formal)
	Ze herinneren ***zich***	They remember

Here are some more common reflexive verbs. As you will see, we always use the reflexive pronoun "zich" with the infinitive:

zich verslapen → to oversleep

zich schamen → to be ashamed/embarrassed

zich vervelen → to be bored

zich voelen → to feel

zich verbazen → to be amazed/surprised

zich gedragen → to behave

zich vermaken → to have fun

zich vergissen → to make a mistake

zich haasten → to hurry

The position of the reflexive pronoun is **right after the main verb** in affirmative sentences:

Ik *verveel* ***me****.* → I am bored.

Zij *voelen* ***zich*** *goed.* → They feel well.

Ouders *vergissen* ***zich*** *soms.* → Parents sometimes make mistakes.

But, in questions and sub-clauses, the reflexive pronoun comes **after the subject**:

Heb ***je je*** *vermaakt?* → Did you enjoy yourself?

Schaamde ***hij zich****?* → Was he ashamed/embarrassed?

Ik vind dat ***jullie je*** *goed gedragen.* → I think you behave well.

Ze zegt dat ***zij zich*** *niets herinnert.* → She says that she remembers nothing.

GRAMMAR: MANIEREN OM BEZIT AAN TE GEVEN WAYS TO INDICATE POSSESSION

Possessive adjectives are the most common way to indicate to who an object belongs. The table below lists the stressed and unstressed forms of the possessive adjectives:

BEZITTELIJKE VOORNAAMWOORDEN (POSSESSIVE ADJECTIVES)			
	Dutch		**English**
	Stressed	**Unstressed**	
Singular	*mijn*	*(m'n)*	my
	jouw	*je*	your
	uw		your (formal)
	zijn	*(z'n)*	his
	haar	*(d'r)*	her
	zijn	*(z'n)*	its
Plural	*ons/onze**		our
	jullie		your
	uw		your (formal)
	hun		their

As you can see, there's an unstressed version for some of the possessive adjectives. The adjectives in brackets are used much less in written Dutch, especially in formal texts, and will be heard more in spoken Dutch.

* *Ons/onze* is the only possessive adjective that changes according to the noun it precedes. Ons is used for neuter nouns that take the article *het*, and *onze* is used for gendered nouns that take *de*, and all nouns in plural, since they also take the article *de*.

Here are some examples:

Dat is ons huis. → That's our house. (because it's *het huis*)

Dat is onze auto. → That's our car. (because it's *de auto*)

Dat zijn onze huizen. → Those are our bicycles. (because it's plural)

Here are some more examples with the other possessive adjectives:

Ik heb last van m'n been. → My leg is bothering me.

Waar zijn je pillen? → Where are your pills?

Uw afspraak is woensdagmiddag om 2 uur. → Your appointment is on Wednesday afternoon at 2 o'clock. (Context is needed to know whether this is for second person singular or plural)

Zijn arm is gebroken. → His arm is broken.

Haar koorts is hoog. → Her fever is high.

Zie je dat oude vliegtuig? Zijn vleugels zijn kapot. → Do you see that old airplane? Its wings are broken.

Hoe laat is jullie operatie? → What time is your surgery?

Hun behandeling loopt morgen af. → Their treatment will finish tomorrow.

Other ways of indicating possession

There are three other ways of indicating to who an object belongs. The first two are almost as common as using the possessive adjectives, the third is quite colloquial, but still useful to know.

1. **Using the preposition *van*, which translates roughly to "the object of", and is followed by the owner's name.**

   De motor van Peter → Peter's motorcycle

   Het paspoort van de toerist → The tourist's passport

   De sokken van de peuter → The toddler's socks

2. **Adding an s to proper names and members of the family, similar to the way it's done in English with 's.**

   Mijn broers fiets → My brother's bicycle

   Marijkes elleboog → Marijke's elbow

3. **The last construction is very colloquial and will only ever be used in spoken Dutch.**

   Udo z'n flat → Udo's apartment

   Claudia d'r vriend → Claudia's (boy)friend

GRAMMAR: DURATIEF **PRESENT CONTINUOUS**

In Dutch we often use the present simple -which you learned to conjugate in Unit 2- to refer to what a person is doing at the time of speaking. In English, we always use the present continuous tense to express this.

However, there is a construction called *duratief*, which is sometimes used to express what a person is doing at the time of speaking, and it's quite easy to learn! It's formed like this: *subject* + *zijn* + *aan het* + infinitive form of the verb.

Here are some examples in the affirmative:

Je bent aan het zeuren. → You're complaining.

De dokter is aan het praten. → The doctor is talking.

De patient is aan het huilen. → The patient is crying.

We zijn aan het winkelen. → We're shopping.

You can never separate *aan het* + infinitive form of the verb, but the subject and *zijn* do need to move to a different position if the sentence is a question, subclause, if the verb is reflexive, or if there's an object in the sentence.

Hij is zich aan het aankleden. → He's getting dressed. (reflexive verb)

Zijn jullie aan het luisteren? → Are you listening? (question)

U bent niet aan het opletten. → You're not paying attention. (negation)

Ik ben de medicijnen aan het innemen. → I'm taking the medicine. (indirect object)

Hij denkt dat ik aan het slapen ben. → He thinks I'm sleeping. (subclause)

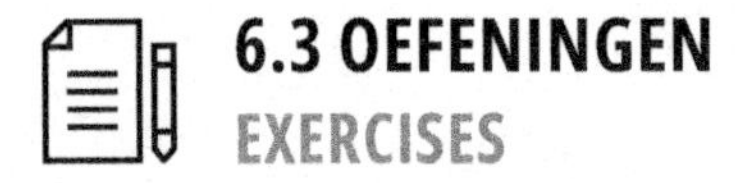

6.3 OEFENINGEN
EXERCISES

1) Complete the table with the names of the body parts listed below. The first one has been filled out as an example.

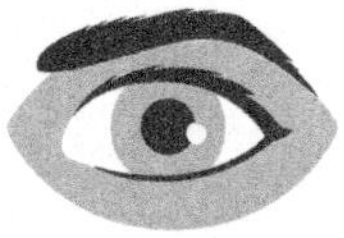 1) (het) oog	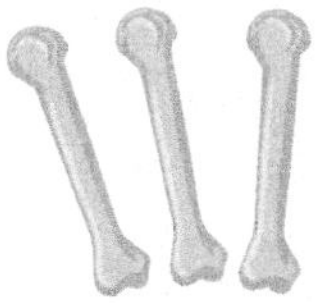 2) ______	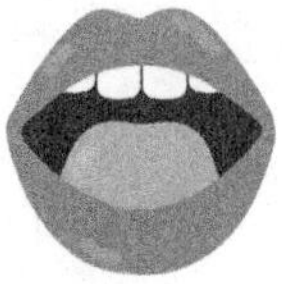 3). ______	 4) ______
 5) ______	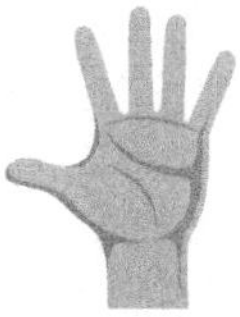 6) ______	 7) ______	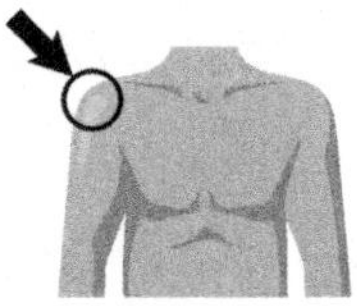 8) ______
 9) ______	 10) ______	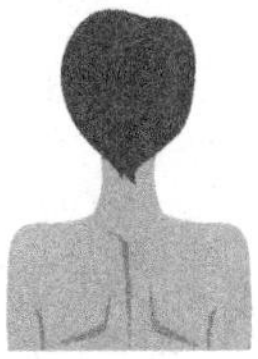 11) ______	 12) ______
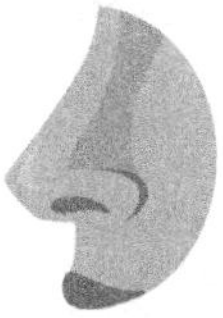 13) ______	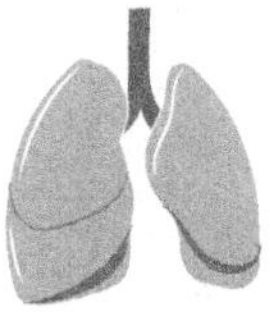 14) ______	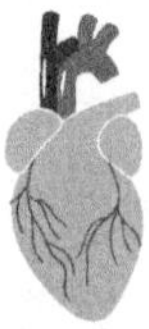 15) ______	 16) ______

2) Fill in the blanks of this short conversation between Anna and her doctor, choosing the correct word from the words listed below. The first one has been filled out as an example.

klachten – medicijnen – pijn – last – kan – zorgen – zwanger – maanden

Anna: *Goedemiddag dokter.*

Dr. de Jong: *Goedemiddag mevrouw ten Haaf. Hoe* ***1)*** ___***kan***___ *ik u helpen?*

Anna: *Ik heb al drie dagen* ***2)*** ____________________ *van mijn buik en hoofdpijn.*

Dr. de Jong: *Oh, dat is vervelend. Heeft u medicijnen tegen de pijn ingenomen?*

Anna: *Nee, want ik ben* ***3)*** ____________________ *en ik weet niet welke medicijnen ik mag innemen.*

Dr. de Jong: *Ah, gefeliciteerd! Dan zijn die* ***4)*** ____________________ *misschien deel van de zwangerschap.*

Anna: *Ja, dat kan, maar ik ben al zes* ***5)*** ____________________ *zwanger en dit is de eerste keer dat ik buikpijn en hoofdpijn heb.*

Dr. de Jong: *Ik begrijp het. Ik ga uw buik onderzoeken. Kunt u hier gaan liggen?*

Anna: *Natuurlijk.*

Dr. de Jong: *Ik ga voorzichtig op uw buik drukken. Doet het hier* ***6)***____________________*?*

Anna: *Ja, een beetje.*

Dr. de Jong: *Okee, u kunt weer gaan zitten. Ik wil nog wat verdere tests doen, maar ik ga u nu al wat* ***7)***____________________ *tegen de pijn voorschrijven.*

Anna: *Oef, dat is fijn. Bedankt dokter! Is het ernstig?*

Dr. de Jong: *Nee hoor, maakt u zich geen* ***8)***____________________*!*

3) Fill in the correct reflexive noun (*me, je, u, zich, ons*). The first one has been filled out as an example.

1) Verveel jij ____**je**____ nooit tijdens de zomervakantie?
(Don't you ever get bored during the summer holidays?)

2) Wij hebben __________ op het feest goed geamuseerd.(We had a good time at the party.)

3) Herinner jij __________ onze lerares wiskunde nog?
(Do you remember our math teacher?)

4) Wij verbazen __________ over de voetbaluitslag.
(We are amazed by the soccer competition results.)

5) De honden hebben __________ heel goed gedragen. (The dogs have behaved very well.)

6) Ik heb __________ nog nooit verslapen. (I have never overslept.)

7) De politieagent heeft __________ vergist. (The police officer made a mistake.)

8) Jij schaamde __________ over je gedrag. (You were embarrassed about your behavior.)

4) Possessive adjectives. Complete the sentence with the possessive adjective that corresponds to the subject in **bold**, choosing from the list: *mijn – jouw – uw – zijn – haar – ons/onze – jullie – hun*. The first one has been filled out as an example.

1) U heeft ______**uw**______ sleutels niet.

2) Wij hebben last van ________________ benen.

3) Sarah heeft pijn in ________________ linkerbeen.

4) Ik mail ________________ dokter met een vraag.

5) Je doet ________________ boodschappen bij de supermarkt.

6) Jullie gaan op maandag naar ________________ opa.

7) We wonen nu 6 maanden in ________________ nieuwe huis.

8) De mensen zijn ________________ fietsen vergeten.

9) Hij viert ________________ verjaardag op zaterdag.

10) U parkeert ________________ auto achter het huis.

5) Expressing possession in other ways. Complete the table with the three ways to express possession. The construction of adding an *s* to the subject in number 6 and 7 aren't possible so those can be left blank. The first one has been filled out as an example.

English translation	Adding an *s*	Possessive adjective	Using *van* (of)
1) Mother's knee	*Moeders knie*	*Haar knie*	*De knie van moeder*
2) Hanneke's neighbors (f)			*De buren van Hanneke*
3) Ahmed's heart		*Zijn hart*	
4) Jan's farm (m)			*De boerderij van Jan*
5) Petra and Karel's car	*Petra en Karels auto*		
6) Piet and my GP	*(not possible)*	*Onze huisarts*	
7) My sister's phone	*(not possible)*		*De telefoon van mijn zus*

6) Present continuous. Write a sentence in the present continuous (subject + *zijn* + aan het + infinitive form) of the verb with elements given. The first one has been filled out as an example.

1) Je / voetballen / in het park

___**Je bent aan het voetballen in het park**___________________________________.

2) De verpleegster / de wond / verbinden

____.

3) De hond / zich / krabben / ?

____.

4) Ik / geen / avondeten / koken

____.

5) Anna / studeren / ?

____.

6) Jij en Klaas / naar de bushalte / rennen

____.

7) De chauffeur / zich haasten

____.

8) De tieners / niet / opletten

____.

6.4 WOORDENLIJST
VOCABULARY LIST

(de) afspraak	appointment, agreement
(de) allergie	allergy
(de) arm	arm
(de) behandeling	treatment
(de) boerderij	farm
(de) buikpijn	stomachache
(de) duizeligheid	dizziness
(de) hand	hand
(de) heup	hip
(de) hoofdpijn	headache
(de) huid	skin
(de) huisarts	general practitioner
(de) keelpijn	sore throat
(de) kiespijn	toothache
(de) klachten	symptoms
(de) koorts	fever
(de) lip	lip
(de) long	lung
(de) meneer	man, Mr.
(de) mevrouw	lady, Mrs.
(de) mond	mouth
(de) peuter	toddler
(de) pijnstiller	painkiller
(de) röntgenfoto	X-ray
(de) rugpijn	backache
(de) schouder	shoulder
(de) spierpijn	sore muscle(s)
(de) spreekkamer	consultation room
(de) teen	toe

(de) tong	tongue
(de) uitslag	rash, test results
(de) verhoging	slight temperature
(de) vinger	finger
(de) vleugel	wing
(de) voet	foot
(de) voetbaluitslag	soccer competition result
(de) wiskunde	mathematics
(de) zalf	ointment
(de) zomervakantie	summer vacation
(de) zorgen	worries
(het) avondeten	dinner
(het) been	leg
(het) bot	bone
(het) feest	party
(het) gezicht	face
(het) haar	hair
(het) hart	heart
(het) linkerbeen	left leg
(het) menselijk lichaam	human body
(het) oog	eye
(het) oor	ear
(het) recept	prescription
(het) rechterbeen	right leg
(het) sproetje	freckle
ach	ah/oh well
bah	yuck, disgusting
besmettelijk	contagious
bezorgd	worried
depressief	depressed
drukken	to press
duizelig	dizzy

erg	awful
erger worden	to get worse
ernstig	severe
gestrest	stressed
gisteren	yesterday
goh	gosh
hè hè	finally!
hierop	on this
huilen	to cry
in de gaten houden	to keep an eye on it
innemen	to ingest
jeetje	gosh
jeuken	to itch
joh	of course
kijken	to look
last hebben van	to suffer from
meevallen	to not be that bad
misselijk	nauseous
moe	tired
nou	well
nou zeg	geez
oei	oof
oh jee	uh oh
ophalen	to pick up
opletten	to pay attention
overgaan	pass
pijnlijk	painful
tjonge jonge	well well
uitstappen	to disembark
verbinden	to connect
vertellen	to tell
verzwikken	sprain

voorschrijven	to prescribe
zeuren	to whine
zich gedragen	to behave
zich haasten	to hurry
zich herinneren	to remember
zich niet lekker voelen	to feel unwell
zich schamen	to be ashamed/embarrassed
zich verbazen	to be amazed, to be surprised
zich vergissen	to make a mistake
zich vermaken	to have fun
zich verslapen	to oversleep
zich vervelen	to be bored
zich voelen	to feel
zich zorgen maken	to worry
zo zo	well, well
zwanger	pregnant

Klaar om te vliegen?

Ready to fly?

7
Deel
Unit

Unit 7 focuses on teaching you vocabulary related to airports and flying, in-flight rules, and geographical features of countries. You'll also learn key modal verbs, how to form the present perfect and the past participle of a group of verbs known as "weak" verbs.

VOCABULARY	PRONUNCIATION
- Vocabulary related to air travel - In-flight rules - Geographical features of countries	- Modal verbs - Conjugation of the present perfect - Past participles of weak verbs

7.1 DUTCH IN CONTEXT: OP HET VLIEGVELD

AT THE AIRPORT

TRACK 26 The Jansen family is going on holiday. Koen, Jessica and their children are at the check-in counter at the airport, about to check-in. Listen to their conversation and read along.

Carolijn: *Goedemorgen! Ik ben Carolijn, uw incheckbalie medewerker vandaag. Mag ik uw paspoorten en vliegtickets alstublieft?*

Koen: *Goedemorgen. Natuurlijk, hier zijn ze. We gaan naar Cusco in Peru. We willen graag bij elkaar zitten, kan dat?*

Carolijn: *Ik zal kijken meneer. Hmm, vluchtnummer KL749. Totaal vier passagiers, toch?*

Jessica: *Dat klopt. Ik wil nog even iets vragen. Mag ik deze fles shampoo in de handbagage meenemen?*

Carolijn: *Mag ik die fles even zien? Oh, daar zit meer dan 100 ml in. Die kunt u niet in uw handbagage doen, want dan halen ze hem er bij de veiligheidscontrole uit.*

Jessica: *Dat is jammer. Dan zal ik de fles nu maar even in mijn koffer doen.*

Carolijn: *Heeft u alle ruimbagage op de band gezet? Bedankt. Hebben de kinderen geen scherpe objecten in hun rugzakken?*

Jessica: *Nee hoor.*

Carolijn: *Hier zijn uw instapkaarten. Uw vlucht heeft geen vertraging. Het gatenummer is C18 en het boarden begint om kwart voor vier. Geniet van uw vlucht en Peru!*

Koen: *Hartelijk bedankt!*

Useful phrases from the conversation:

We willen graag bij elkaar zitten, kan dat? → We'd like to sit together, is that possible?

Totaal vier passagiers, toch? → A total of four passengers, right?

Mag ik deze fles shampoo in de handbagage meenemen? → May I take this bottle of shampoo in my hand luggage?

Die kunt u niet in uw handbagage doen. → You can't put that in your hand luggage.

Heeft u alle ruimbagage op de band gezet? → Have you put all of your check-in luggage on the conveyor belt?

WOORDENLIJST VOOR OP HET VLIEGVELD (AIRPORT VOCABULARY)	
Dutch	**English**
(het) vliegveld, (de) luchthaven	airport
(de) landingsbaan	landing strip
(de) aankomsthal	arrival hall
(de) vertrekhal	departure hall
(de) incheckbalie	check-in counter
(het) visum	visa
(de) douane	customs
(de) veiligheidscontrole	security check
(het) vliegtuig	airplane
(de) luchtvaartmaatschappij	airline
(het) paspoort	passport
(de) bestemming	destination
(het) vliegticket	flight ticket
(de) vlucht	flight
(de) bagage	luggage

(de) handbagage	hand luggage
(de) koffer	suitcase
(de) rugzak	backpack
(de) instapkaart	boarding pass
(het) boekingsnummer	booking number
(de) piloot	pilot
(de) steward(ess)	air host(ess)
(het) cabinepersoneel	cabin crew
(de) passagier	passenger
(de) tussenstop	stopover
(het) stoelnummer	seat number
(de) riem	seatbelt
(de) nooduitgang	emergency exit
(de) toilet	restroom
(de) maaltijd	meal
(de) vertraging	delay
afscheid nemen	to say goodbye
vertrekken	to leave
aankomen	to arrive
landen	to land
opstijgen	to take off
inchecken	to check-in
boarden	to board
instappen	to get in
missen	to miss
slapen	to sleep

DUTCH IN CONTEXT: BELANGRIJKE REGELS TIJDENS UW VLUCHT
IMPORTANT RULES DURING YOUR FLIGHT

Flying is subject to a number of rules which are important for all passengers to know and comply with to ensure flight safety for everyone. In the table below, we've listed several rules using the modal verbs *willen* (to want), *kunnen* (can, to be able to), *mogen* (may/to be allowed to), *moeten*, (to have to/must), and *niet hoeven* (not have an obligation to do something).

BELANGRIJKE REGELS TIJDENS EEN VLUCHT (IMPORTANT RULES DURING A FLIGHT)	
Dutch	**English**
- *Passagiers moeten hun riem omhebben tijdens het opstijgen en landen.*	- Passengers must wear their seatbelts during take-off and landing.
- *Reizigers hoeven niet de hele vlucht hun riem om te hebben.*	- Travelers don't have to wear their seatbelts throughout the entire flight.
- *Laptops mogen gebruikt worden tijdens de vlucht.*	- Laptops may be used during the flight.
- *Passagiers die het toilet willen gebruiken, moeten dat doen na het opstijgen en voor het landen.*	- Passengers who want to use the restroom must do so after taking off and before landing.
- *Reizigers kunnen hun schoenen uitdoen tijdens de vlucht.*	- Travelers may take off their shoes during the flight.
- *Passagiers ouder dan 18 jaar mogen tijdens de vlucht alcoholische dranken bestellen.*	- Passengers over 18 years old are allowed to order alcoholic beverages during the flight.
- *Alle reizigers moeten hun instapkaart laten scannen bij het instappen.*	- All passengers must have their boarding pass scanned when boarding.

INTERESSANTE WEETJES

The Netherlands is well known for having extensive parts of its surface areas below sea level. But did you know exactly how much of the country is below sea level? Have a look at the map on the right, it might surprise you!

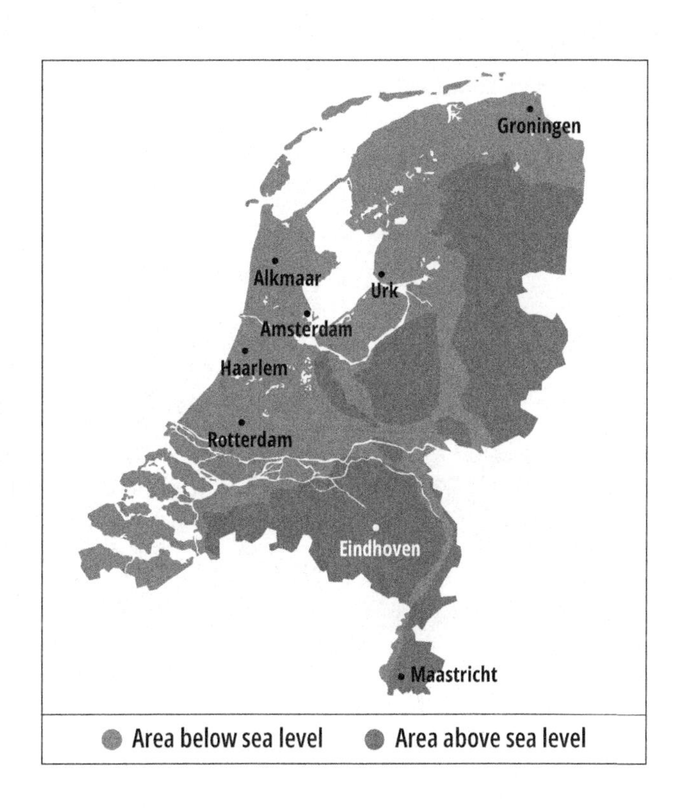

LANDSCHAPSKENMERKEN (GEOGRAPHICAL FEATURES)			
 *(de) berg* (mountain)	 *(de) heuvel* (hill)	 *(het) bos* (forest)	 *(de) vallei* (valley)
 *(het) meer* (lake)	 *(de) rivier* (river)	 *(de) zee* sea	 *(het) strand* beach
 *(de) woestijn* (desert)	 *(het) eiland* (island)	 *(de) waterval* (waterfall)	 *(de) kust* (the coast)

DUTCH IN CONTEXT: WAT EEN MOOI LAND! WHAT A BEAUTIFUL COUNTRY!

TRACK 27 The Jansen family have arrived in Cusco and are in a taxi on the way to their hotel. They're talking to their driver Juan about the differences between Peru and the Netherlands. Listen to their conversation and read along.

Juan:	*Welkom in Cusco! Wat vindt u ervan?*
Koen:	*Oh, het is prachtig! Zo anders dan Nederland!*
Juan:	*Dat kan ik me voorstellen. Zijn er ook bergen in Nederland?*
Jessica:	*Haha, nee hoor, de hoogste berg is maar 322 meter hoog.*
Juan:	*322 meter! Dat is geen berg, dat is een heuvel!*
Jessica:	*Ja, inderdaad. Zijn er ook veel bossen in Cusco?*
Juan:	*Zeker wel. Er zijn watervallen, valleien, meren en rivieren. Maar als u strand en zee wilt, moet u naar de kust, bijvoorbeeld naar Lima.*
Koen:	*Je kan niet alles hebben!*

Useful phrases from the conversation:

Zo anders dan Nederland! → Very different from the Netherlands!

Dat kan ik me voorstellen. → I can imagine.

De hoogste berg is maar 322 meter hoog. → The highest mountain is only 322 meters high.

Ja, inderdaad. → Yes, exactly.

Je kan niet alles hebben! → You can't have it all!

7.2 GRAMMAR: HULPWERKWOORDEN

MODAL VERBS

The following four modal verbs are used very frequently in Dutch:

willen → to want

kunnen → to be able to (or the verb can)

mogen → to be allowed to (or the verb may)

moeten → to have to (or the verb must)

Their conjugation in the present tense is irregular, so here's a full overview:

PERSONAL PRONOUNS	WILLEN (TO WANT)	KUNNEN (CAN / TO BE ABLE TO)	MOGEN (MAY / TO BE ALLOWED)	MOETEN (MUST / TO HAVE TO)
ik	*wil*	*kan*	*mag*	*moet*
je, jij, u	*wil / wilt**	*kan / kunt**	*mag*	*moet*
hij, zij, het	*wil*	*kan*	*mag*	*moet*
we, wij	*willen*	*kunnen*	*mogen*	*moeten*
jullie u	*willen* *wil / wilt**	*kunnen*	*mogen*	*moeten*
ze, zij	*willen*	*kunnen*	*mogen*	*moeten*

* *wilt* and *kunt* are more formal than *wil*, and *kan.*

These modal verbs are usually combined with another verb. The second verb is put at the very end of the sentence and is always in the infinitive form.

Kunt u me helpen? → Can you help me?

Mogen we hier fietsen? → May we (are we allowed) to cycle here?

Ik kan niet autorijden. → I can't drive.

Often when these modal verbs are used with the verbs *hebben* (to have), *gaan* (to go) or *doen* (to do), those verbs are usually omitted but their meaning is still implied. Examples with *hebben*:

Wij willen een kopje koffie. → We want (to have) a cup of coffee.

But: *Wij willen een kopje thee bestellen.* → We want to order a cup of tea.

Examples with *gaan*:

Ik moet naar het stadhuis. → I have to (go to) the town hall.

But: *Ik moet naar Spanje vliegen.* → I have to fly to Spain.

Examples with *doen*:

Ze kunnen het goed. → They can do it well (as in, they're good at it).

But: *Ze kunnen goed koken.* → They can cook well.

Additional rules about the use of these modal verbs

Please note that the modal verb is always the second item in affirmative sentences and that the verb in the infinitive always comes at the very end of the sentence.

Ik wil een nieuwe jurk kopen. → I want to buy a new dress.

Ze gaat televisie kijken. → She is going to watch television.

Zij willen wat eten. → They want something to eat.

To turn the above affirmative sentences into questions, simply invert the subject and the modal verb:

Wil ik een nieuwe jurk kopen? → Do I want to buy a new dress?

Gaat ze televisie kijken? → Is she going to watch television?

Willen zij wat eten? → Do they want something to eat?

Other modal verbs that are followed by the preposition *te*

There is also a group of verbs that can be used together with an infinitive, but in these cases the preposition *te* will have to be inserted before the infinitive. These modal verbs are:

proberen → to try

vergeten → to forget

staan → to stand, to be located

zitten → to be (sit)

beginnen → to start

beloven → to promise

Look at the following examples and their translation:

1. *Zij probeert te helpen* → She is trying to help.
2. *Wij vergeten hem te bellen.* → We forget to call him.
3. *Jij staat te wachten.* → You are waiting (probaby in a standing position).
4. *U zit te lezen.* → You are reading (probaby in a sitting position).
5. *De auto begint te rijden.* → The car starts to drive.
6. *Ik beloof haar te helpen.* → I promise to help her.

Moeten or _hoeven_, that is the question.

Niet hoeven is used when there's no obligation to do something. You need to use the preposition *te* in front of the main verb. *Moeten* is used when there *is* an obligation to do something. Remember that it doesn't come with the preposition *te*.

U hoeft niet te bellen. → You don't have to come.

Jullie hoeven niet ver te fietsen. → You don't have to cycle far.

U moet de brief goed lezen. → You have to read the letter carefully.

Jullie moeten direct komen. → You have to come immediately.

Je moet dat niet doen. → You mustn't do that.

GRAMMAR: VERVOEGING VAN DE VOLTOOID TEGENWOORDIGE TIJD
CONJUGATION OF THE PRESENT PERFECT

It's time to learn the Dutch equivalent of the present perfect! The reason we're teaching you this before we get to the Dutch equivalent of the simple past, is because the present perfect is very often used to refer to past events in cases where we'd use a simple past in English.

The basic conjugation of the Dutch present perfect is simple and similar to the English present perfect, since it uses an auxiliary verb (usually *hebben*, less often *zijn*, more on that in Unit 8) and a past participle. Like in English, there are regular and irregular past participles. In this unit, we'll only use past participles of the category known as "weak verbs", which are regular. The reason they're called "weak" is because they do not undergo any vowel changes.

VERVOEGING VAN WANDELEN IN DE VOLTOOID TEGENWOORDIGE TIJD (CONJUGATION OF TO STROLL IN THE PRESENT PERFECT)	
Ik heb gewandeld	I have strolled
Jij hebt gewandeld	You have strolled
U hebt/heeft gewandeld	You have strolled
Hij/zij/het heeft gewandeld	He/she has strolled
Wij hebben gewandeld	We have strolled
Jullie hebben gewandeld	You have strolled
Zij hebben gewandeld	They have strolled

Since the above only show the word order for affirmative sentences, here are some examples of negative sentences and questions:

Negative sentences:

De kinderen hebben niet gespeeld. → The children didn't play/haven't played.

Mijn opa en oma hebben niet gereisd. → My grandparents didn't travel/haven't traveled.

De toeristen hebben niet gewacht. → The tourists didn't wait/haven't waited.

Ik heb geen mensen gebeld. → I didn't call/haven't called any people.

Questions:

Heeft haar zus gedanst? → Did her sister dance? / Has her sister danced?

Waarom heeft u gemaild? → Why did you send an email? / Why have you emailed?

Heeft het publiek goed geluisterd? → Did the audience listen properly? / Has the audience listened properly?

Hoe laat hebben ze naar jouw huis gebeld? → What time did they call your house? / What time have they called your house?

As you can see from the above examples, the negation (whether it's *niet* or *geen* + noun) always follows the auxiliary verb and the past participle comes at the end of the sentence.As for questions, the order is: auxiliary verb + subject + (objects) + past participle.

GRAMMAR: VOLTOOID DEELWOORD VAN ZWAKKE WERKWOORDEN

PAST PARTICIPLES OF WEAK VERBS

The way the past participles of Dutch verbs are formed can be divided into the following three categories:

1. Weak verbs *ge + stem + t or d*	**2.** Strong verbs *ge + verb*	**3.** Irregular verbs *(no rule)*

In order not to overwhelm you, we'll only be learning the conjugation of the first group in this unit, the other two categories will be treated in Unit 8. The good news is that most Dutch verbs fall into the first category.

This is how you form the past participle of weak verbs:

1. Find the stem of the verb (usually this means just removing the *-en* from the end, if the verb has an open vowel sound you will have to double the vowel).
2. For the verb *wandelen*, the stem is *wandel*.
3. Add *ge-* to the stem. In this case: *gewandel-*
4. Add a *-t* or a *-d* at the end of the stem, in this case: *gewandeld*.

Fortunately, there is a rule you can memorize to know when you add a *-t* and when you add a *-d* at the end of the verb: the *-t* is added when the stem of the verb ends in: **p, t, k, s, f, ch** and **x**. Even if the verb ends on a *d*, it effectively sounds like a *t*, so it's common for even native speakers to make spelling mistakes with past participles. To help avoid this, Dutch children are taught the mnemonic *'t kofschip*, which contains all the letters mentioned above. There's even a mnemonic in English: *soft ketchup*.

Here are some examples which will help you get the hang of it:

VOORBEELDEN VAN VOLTOOIDE DEELWOORDEN VAN ZWAKKE WERKWOORDEN (EXAMPLES OF PAST PARTICIPLES OF WEAK VERBS)			
Infinitive	**Stem**	**Past participle**	**English translation**
kleuren	*kleur*	*gekleurd*	to color
stoppen	*stop (only 1 p)*	*gestopt*	to stop
maken	*maak (add extra a)*	*gemaakt*	to make
fietsen	*fiets*	*gefietst*	to cycle
branden	*brand*	*gebrand**	to burn
redden	*red (only 1 d)*	*gered**	to save
regenen	*regen*	*geregend*	to rain
reizen	*reis (z → s)*	*gereisd*	to travel
leven	*leef (+e; v → f)*	*geleefd*	to live
testen	*test*	*getest*	to test

* When the stem of the verb ends in -t or -d, don't add another t or d.

7.3 OEFENINGEN
EXERCISES

1) Airport vocabulary. Choose the right word from the two options given. The first one has been filled out as an example.

1) Hallo, ik heb een vraag: waar is de (**vertrekhal**/visum)?
2) Onze (bestemming/nooduitgang) is New York
3) Oh nee! Uw vliegtuig heeft (douane/vertraging)!
4) U moet uiterlijk om kwart over een (inchecken/paspoorten).
5) Dames en heren, we gaan landen, u moet nu uw (aankomsthal/riem) omdoen.
6) Sorry mevrouw, uw (vlucht/koffer) weegt 5 kilo te veel.
7) Snel! Het vliegtuig gaat bijna (vertrekken/instappen)!
8) Waar is het (toilet/stoelnummer) alstublieft?

2) Geographical features. The table below has the 12 geographical features that you learned in this unit, however, 7 out of the 12 names have been mixed up. Find the incorrectly labeled images and write the correct name instead.

1) *de berg*	**2)** *de heuvel*	**3)** *het bos*	**4)** *de vallei*
5) *het meer*	**6)** *de rivier*	**7)** *de zee*	**8)** *het strand*
9) *de woestijn*	**10)** *het eiland*	**11)** *de waterval*	**12)** *de kust*

3) Questions and answers with modal verbs. Match the questions with the correct answers. The first one has been filled out as an example.

	Questions	Answers
D	**1)** Kan je je arm bewegen?	**a)** Ja, dat moet hij doen.
	2) Willen jullie suiker in jullie thee?	**b)** Ja, doe ze maar uit.
	3) Moet de schoonmaker de ramen schoonmaken?	**c)** Ja, vraagt u maar.
	4) Mogen wij iets vragen?	**d)** Ja, dat kan ik.
	5) Moeten we onze schoenen uitdoen?	**e)** Ja, natuurlijk. Wil je ook melk en suiker?
	6) Kun je autorijden?	**f)** Nee, dat willen we niet.
	7) Wil Sarah de pillen innemen?	**g)** Nee, ik kan alleen fietsen
	8) Mag ik nog een kopje koffie?	**h)** Nee, dat wil ze niet.

4) Modal verbs. Complete the sentences with the correct conjugation in the present tense of the modal verb given. The first one has been filled out as an example.

1) Ik ___**wil**___ op woensdag naar de universiteit fietsen. (willen)

2) ________________ je hier hardlopen? (mogen)

3) Zij ________________ heel goed tekenen. (kunnen) (third person plural)

4) Ik ________________ morgen mijn boeken inleveren bij de bibliotheek. (moeten).

5) Hij ________________ morgenmiddag niet komen. (kunnen)

6) ________________ mijn dochter een koekje pakken? (mogen)

7) De kinderen ________________ nog even buiten spelen. (willen)

8) We ________________ vanavond of morgenmiddag naar de film gaan. (kunnen)

9) Jullie ________________ eerst je huiswerk afmaken voordat jullie tv ________________ kijken. (moeten / mogen)

11) Zij ________________ graag nog een toetje bestellen. (willen) (third person singular)

5) Present perfect. Write a sentence in the present perfect tense with the elements given. Pay special attention to the word order. The first one has been filled out as an example.

1) Wij / maken / een nieuwe afspraak met de dokter.

Answer: Wij hebben een nieuwe afspraak met de dokter gemaakt.

2) Ik / niet geloven / het excuus

____.

3) Klaartje / reizen / naar Azië / ?

____.

4) Het / regenen / de hele nacht

____.

5) Mijn zus / lezen / veel

____.

6) U / dansen / gisteren / ?

____.

7) De brandweer / redden / de hond

____.

8) De ouders / niet luisteren / naar de directrice

____.

9) Het meisje / kleuren / de tekening

____.

10) Jij / mailen / ons / ?

____.

6) Past participle of weak verbs. Change the infinitive of the weak verbs listed into the past participle by adding ge- in front of the verb and -t or -d behind the verb. The first one has been filled out as an example.

1) praten ______**gepraat**______.

2) missen ________________.

3) werken ________________.

4) vragen ________________.

5) delen ________________.

6) leven ________________.

7) zetten ________________.

8) verven ________________.

9) leggen ________________.

10) leren ________________.

7.4 WOORDENLIJST
VOCABULARY LIST

(de) aankomsthal	arrival hall
(de) bagage	luggage
(de) berg	mountain
(de) bestemming	destination
(de) brandweer	firefighters
(de) douane	customs
(de) drank	beverage
(de) handbagage	hand luggage
(de) heuvel	hill
(de) incheckbalie	check-in counter
(de) instapkaart	boarding pass
(de) koffer	suitcase
(de) kust	coast
(de) landingsbaan	landing strip
(de) luchtvaartmaatschappij	airline
(de) maaltijd	meal
(de) nooduitgang	emergency exit
(de) passagier	passenger
(de) piloot	pilot
(de) reiziger	traveler
(de) riem	seatbelt
(de) rivier	river
(de) schoonmaker	the cleaner
(de) steward(ess)	air host(ess)
(de) toilet	restroom
(de) tussenstop	stopover
(de) vallei	valley
(de) veiligheidscontrole	security check
(de) vertraging	delay

(de) vertrekhal	departure hall
(de) vlucht	flight
(de) waterval	waterfall
(de) woestijn	desert
(de) zee	sea
(het) boekingsnummer	booking number
(het) bos	forest
(het) cabinepersoneel	cabin crew
(het) eiland	island
(het) koekje	cookie
(het) meer	lake
(het) paspoort	passport
(het) stadhuis	town hall
(het) stoelnummer	seat number
(het) strand	beach
(het) toetje	dessert
(het) visum	visa
(het) vliegticket	flight ticket
(het) vliegtuig	airplane
(het) vliegveld, *(de) luchthaven*	airport
aankomen	to arrive
afscheid nemen	to say goodbye
beloven	to promise
bewegen	to move
bijvoorbeeld	for example
boarden	to board
branden	to burn
dansen	to dance
gebruiken	to use
geloven	to believe
graag	preferably

hardlopen	to jog
hoog	high
inchecken	to check-in
inderdaad	exactly
instappen	to get in
kleuren	to color
kunnen	to be able to
landen	to land
leggen	to put
leren	to learn
leven	to live
luisteren	to listen
missen	to miss
moeten	to have to
mogen	to be allowed to
niet hoeven	to not have an obligation
opstijgen	to take off
prachtig	beautiful
proberen	to try
redden	to save
reizen	to travel
slapen	to sleep
tekenen	to draw
vergeten	to forget
vertrekken	to leave
verven	to paint
voorstellen	to imagine, to propose (an idea), to introduce someone
wandelen	to stroll, hike
zetten	to put

Heb je die film gezien?

Have you seen that movie?

8
Deel
Unit

Unit 8 focuses on teaching you how to use the verb *laten*, and the vocabulary you'll need to talk about movies and books, such as the names of the different genres and adjectives to use to describe them. You'll also learn the common past participles of strong and irregular verbs, more about which auxiliary verb to use for the present perfect (*hebben* or *zijn*), and what separable verbs are and how to use them.

VOCABULARY	GRAMMAR
- Vocabulary to talk about books and films and to express your opinion about them - The verb *laten*	- *Hebben* or *zijn* as auxiliary verbs for the present perfect - Past participles of strong and irregular verbs - Separable verbs

8.1 DUTCH IN CONTEXT: HEB JE DIE FILM GEZIEN?

HAVE YOU SEEN THAT MOVIE?

TRACK 28 Kim and Pepijn are best friends and love going to the cinema. Listen and read along with their conversation below where they're discussing movies.

Pepijn: *Kimmetje! Alles goed?*

Kim: *Ja hoor! Hé, laten we vanavond naar de bioscoop gaan!*

Pepijn: *Leuk! Ben je weleens in het Tuschinski Theater geweest?*

Kim: *Nee, nog nooit! Wat draait daar?*

Pepijn: *Even kijken. Vanavond draaien ze Turks Fruit, de klassieker van Paul Verhoeven!*

Kim: *Cool! Dat is een hele goede regisseur, toch?*

Pepijn: *Ontzettend goed!*

Kim: *Wat voor soort film is het?*

Pepijn: *Tsja, drama volgens mij.*

Kim: *Oké, klinkt goed. Kan jij de kaartjes reserveren?*

Pepijn: *Ja hoor, ik zie je straks!*

WOORDENLIJST VOOR FILMS (MOVIE VOCABULARY)			
Dutch	**English**	**Dutch**	**English**
(de) documentaire	documentary	*(het) verhaal*	story
(de) komedie	comedy	*(het) begin*	beginning
(de) actiefilm	action movie	*(het) einde*	end
(de) misdaadfilm	crime movie	*spannend*	exciting, thrilling
(de) bioscoop	cinema	*romantisch*	romantic
(het) kaartje	ticket	*eng*	scary
(de) acteur	actor	*grappig*	funny
(de) actrice	actress	*leuk*	fun
(de) rol	roll	*geweldig*	awesome
(de) regisseur	director	*emotioneel*	emotional
(de) recensie	review	*dramatisch*	dramatic

Useful phrases from the conversation:

Hé, laten we vanavond naar de bioscoop gaan! → Hey, let's go to the movies tonight!

Wat draait daar? → What's playing there?

Even kijken. → Let me see.

Wat voor soort film is het? → What kind of movie is it?

Tsja, drama volgens mij. → Hmm, drama I think.

DUTCH IN CONTEXT: IN DE BIBLIOTHEEK AT THE LIBRARY

TRACK 29 Karel is an avid reader and active member of his local library in the Dutch city of Utrecht. Listen and read along with the conversation between him and a library staff member, Lieke.

Karel: *Goedemorgen! Mag ik even iets vragen?*

Lieke: *Natuurlijk meneer.*

Karel: *Ik wil graag deze zes boeken lenen, maar wat is de leentermijn?*

Lieke: *De standaard leentermijn is drie weken en die kunt u nog één keer voor drie weken verlengen.*

Karel: *Ah, perfect. Kan ik de boeken ook door iemand anders laten terugbrengen?*

Lieke: *Jazeker.*

Karel: *Dat is fijn. Geldt hetzelfde trouwens voor tijdschriften?*

Lieke: *Nee, de leentermijn voor tijdschriften is maar één week en die kunt u niet verlengen.*

Karel: *Oké, hartelijk bedankt mevrouw!*

Lieke: *U mag gewoon Lieke zeggen hoor!*

Karel: *Oh, oké. Sorry. Bedankt Lieke!*

WOORDENLIJST VOOR BIBLIOTHEEK (LIBRARY VOCABULARY)			
Dutch	**English**	**Dutch**	**English**
(de) bibliotheek	library	*(het) lidmaatschap*	membership
(de) auteur	author	*(de) leentermijn*	loan term
(het) woordenboek	dictionary	*uitleggen*	to explain
(het) luisterboek	audiobook	*lenen*	to lend
(het) tijdschrift	magazine	*terugbrengen*	to return
(het) lid	member	*verlengen*	to extend
(het) abonnement	subscription	*gelden*	to be valid

Useful phrases from the conversation:

Mag ik even iets vragen? → Can I ask you a quick question?

Kan ik de boeken ook door iemand anders laten terugbrengen? → Can I also have someone else return the books?

Geldt hetzelfde voor tijdschriften? → Is it the same for magazines?

U mag gewoon Lieke zeggen hoor! → You can just call me Lieke, you know.

Het werkwoord laten (the verb *laten*)

Both this and the previous conversation contained the verb laten, but both with a different meaning. Laten is a very versatile verb, especially when combined with other prepositions, adjectives or other verbs, so we've listed some examples to illustrate its different meanings in the table below.

HET WERKWOORD LATEN (THE VERB "LATEN")	
Dutch	English
Laat *me alleen.*	**Leave** me alone.
Laten *we naar de bioscoop gaan!*	**Let's** go to the movies. (*laten we* is usually used to say "let's")
Zij heeft haar boek op school ***gelaten****.*	She **left** her book at school.
Ik heb mijn nagels ***laten*** *lakken.*	I **got** my nails done. (here, laten + verb has the meaning of getting something done)

8.2 GRAMMAR: VOLTOOID DEELWOORDEN VAN STERKE EN ONREGELMATIGE WERKWOORDEN

PAST PARTICIPLES FOR STRONG AND IRREGULAR VERBS

In Unit 7, we introduced the present perfect, but you learned only one of the three types of past participles: the weak verbs. Now it's time to learn how to form the past participle of strong verbs and to learn some of the most common irregular verbs:

Here's the overview of the past participle formation again:

1. Weak verbs	**2.** Strong verbs	**3.** Irregular verbs
ge + stem + t or d	*ge + verb*	*(no rule)*

2. Strong verbs

In most cases, the past participle of strong verbs is formed by adding the prefix *ge-* to the verb, and keeping the *-en* at the end (unlike with weak verbs, where you remove the *-en*.)
However, the stem of many verbs experiences a vowel change in the stem, so it's really just a case of learning the strong verbs as you come across them.

Strong verbs without vowel changes in the past participle:

komen (to come) → *gekomen*

lezen (to read) → *gelezen*

gaan (to go) → *gegaan*

Strong verbs with vowel changes in the past participle:

spreken (to speak) → *gesproken*

kijken (to watch) → *gekeken*

nemen (to take) → *genomen*

Here are ten common past participles of strong verbs to get started with:

VOORBEELDEN VAN VOLTOOID DEELWOORDEN VAN STERKE WERKWOORDEN (EXAMPLES OF PAST PARTICIPLES OF STRONG VERBS)		
Infinitive	**Past participle**	**English translation**
bijten	*gebeten*	to bite
dragen	*gedragen*	to carry
drinken	*gedronken*	to drink
eten	*gegeten*	to eat
lopen	*gelopen*	to walk
krijgen	*gekregen*	to receive
rijden	*gereden*	to drive
schrijven	*geschreven*	to write
slapen	*geslapen*	to sleep
weten	*geweten*	to know

Lastly, verbs that start with other prefixes such as *ver-*, *be-*, *ont-*, usually don't take the prefix *ge-* at all.

verliezen (to lose) → *verloren*	*verslaan* (to defeat) → *verslagen*

3. Irregular verbs

Now it's time to have a look at verbs that have completely irregular past participles. The good news is that the list isn't that long!

The list below contains the most common irregular verbs you'll need for now.

VOORBEELDEN VAN VOLTOOIDE DEELWOORDEN VAN STERKE WERKWOORDEN (EXAMPLES OF PAST PARTICIPLES OF STRONG VERBS)		
Infinitive	**Past participle**	**English translation**
brengen	*gebracht*	to bring
denken	*gedacht*	to think
doen	*gedaan*	to do
hebben	*gehad*	to have
kopen	*gekocht*	to buy
slaan	*geslagen*	to hit
staan	*gestaan*	to stand
zien	*gezien*	to see
zijn	*geweest*	to be
zoeken	*gezocht*	to search

GRAMMAR: HULPWERKWOORDEN VOOR DE VOLTOOID TEGENWOORDIGE TIJD
AUXILIARY VERBS FOR THE PRESENT PERFECT

We have almost finished teaching you the pesky present perfect in Dutch, but there's this last section to delve a bit more deeply into it: the auxiliary verb. In English, there is only one auxiliary verb for the present perfect (to have), and in Unit 7 you learned that one of the auxiliary verbs to use for the present perfect in Dutch is "*hebben*". However, some verbs use the verb "*zijn*" (to be), and some verbs that can use both. The choice of which to use will depend on the context of the sentence.

1. Common verbs that always use *zijn* to make the perfect tense:

INFINITIVE	EXAMPLE IN THE PRESENT PERFECT	ENGLISH TRANSLATION OF THE EXAMPLE
zijn	*Ik ben geweest.*	I have been.
blijven	*Wij zijn gebleven.*	We have stayed.
komen	*Het pakket is niet gekomen.*	The package hasn't come.
gaan	*Is je vriend gegaan?*	Did your friend go?
beginnen	*De film is begonnen.*	The movie has started.
stoppen	*U bent gestopt.*	You have stopped.
vertrekken	*De trein is vertrokken.*	The train has left.
verhuizen	*Ben je al verhuisd?*	Have you moved yet?
vallen	*Het glas is gevallen.*	The glass has fallen.
worden	*Mijn opa is 94 geworden.*	My grandfather turned 94.
scheiden	*Haar ouders zijn net gescheiden.*	Her parents have just divorced.
sterven	*Mijn hond is gestorven.*	My dog has died.
zoeken	*Julle hebben niet gezocht.*	You haven't searched.

2. There is also a group of verbs that sometimes uses *hebben* and sometimes *zijn* in the perfect tense.

These verbs usually indicate some sort of motion. *Zijn* is used when there is an indication of direction or destination. *Hebben* is used when there is no direction, and the emphasis is more on the movement itself. Here are some examples.

lopen — to walk
De oude vrouw ***is*** *tot de brievenbus* ***gelopen***. — The old woman walked to the post box.
Zij ***heeft*** *een uur in het stadscentrum* ***gelopen***. — She walked in the city center for an hour.

wandelen — to stroll, hike
Ik ***ben*** *naar de rivier* ***gewandeld***. — I walked to the river.
Ik ***heb*** *gisteren in het bos* ***gewandeld***. — Yesterday, I have walked in the forest.

rijden	to drive
Zij ***zijn*** *naar Rotterdam* ***gereden****.*	They drove to Rotterdam.
Jullie ***hebben*** *wat rond de stad* ***gereden****.*	You drove around the city for a while.
vliegen	to fly
We ***zijn*** *naar Madrid* ***gevlogen****.*	We flew to Madrid.
Ik ***heb*** *nog nooit eerder* ***gevlogen****.*	I have never flown before.
fietsen	to cycle
Zij ***is*** *naar de universiteit* ***gefietst****.*	She cycled to the university.
Hij ***heeft*** *heel snel* ***gefietst****.*	He has cycled very fast.
rennen	to run
Jij ***bent*** *eerst naar huis* ***gerend****.*	You ran home first
U ***heeft*** *gisteren veel* ***gerend****.*	You have run a lot yesterday.

GRAMMAR: SCHEIDBARE WERKWOORDEN SEPARABLE VERBS

By now, you've already come across verbs with some prefixes like *be-*, *her-*, *ont-*, *ver-* and *er-*. These are all fixed prefixes, which means that they can never be separated from the verb. However, in Dutch there are also many verbs with prefixes that have to be separated from the verb in most conjugations. These verbs are often made up of a preposition like out, in, by or with, with is added before the verb as a prefix.

Here are some useful examples:

1. *Opbellen* is a combination of *op* + *bellen* (to call on the phone)
2. *Ophangen* is a combination of *op* + *hangen* (to end a phone call)
3. *Binnenkomen* is a combination of *binnen* + *komen* (to enter)
4. *Meebrengen* is a combination of *mee* + *brengen* (to bring along)
5. *Afwassen* is a combination of *af* + *wassen* (to wash the dishes)
6. *Aansteken* is a combination of *aan* + *steken* (to light a fire or cigarette)
7. *Uitproberen* is a combination of *uit* + *proberen* (to try out)
8. *Weggaan* is a combination of *weg* + *gaan* (to go away)

9. *Nadenken* is a combination of *na* + *denken* (to think about)

10. *Wegzetten* is a combination of *weg* + *zetten* (to put away)

Sometimes the prefix is an adverb or adjective in combination with a verb:

1. *Schoonmaken* is a combination of *schoon* + *maken* (to clean)

2. *Samenwerken* is a combination of *samen* + *werken* (collaborate)

The reason these verbs are called separable is that when the verb is conjugated, the prefix is separated from the main verb. When the separable verb is the main verb and it is in the present tense or simple past tense. the prefix is moved all the way to the end of the sentence.

*Hij **belt** zijn vriend **op**.*	He's phoning his friend.
***Hou** je mijn tas **vast**?*	Will you hold my bag?
*Zij **hangt** haar jas **op**.*	She hangs up her coat.
***Breng** je bloemen voor je moeder **mee**?*	Will you bring flowers for your mom?

However: when using the infinitive of the separable verb in combination with a modal verb, the two parts stay together:

*Wij moeten nu **weggaan**.*	We have to leave now.
*Wij zullen **afwassen**.*	We will do the dishes.
*Ik zal een nieuwe dieet **uitproberen**.*	I will try out a new dieet.

In the present perfect tense, the past participle has to be placed at the end of a sentence. The past participle for separable verbs is formed by adding *ge-* in between the prefix and the original verb (in infinitive form):

*Ik heb mijn jas **opgehangen**.*	I have hung up my coat.
*Zij hebben voor ons **afgewassen**.*	They have done the dishes for us.
*Is hij gisteren eerder **weggegaan**?*	Did he leave earlier yesterday?

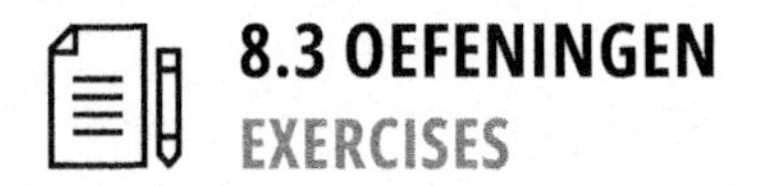

8.3 OEFENINGEN
EXERCISES

1) Film and library vocabulary. Fill in the correct missing word from the options given in the box below. The first one has been filled out as an example.

kaartjes / laten / grappig / eng / recensie / auteurs / lid / terugbrengen / begin / **actrice**

1) Welke ___actrice___ vind je leuker: Kirsten Dunst of Angelina Jolie?

2) Die komedie is echt heel ____________.

3) Eén van mijn favoriete Nederlandse ____________ is Jan Terlouw.

4) ____________ dit weekend naar het theater gaan!

5) ik hou niet van horror films, die zijn heel ____________.

6) Hoeveel kosten de ____________ voor de matineefilm?

7) Wanneer moeten we deze boeken ____________?

8) Het ____________ van deze film is nogal saai, maar daarna wordt het spannend.

9) Mijn oom kan geen boeken lenen want hij is geen ____________ van de bibliotheek.

10) Volgens de ____________ is de James Bond film heel goed!

2) From present to present perfect. The sentences below are in the present tense. Rewrite them in the present perfect tense, changing the verb in bold. Pay attention to the conjugation of the past participle of the verb, as it could be weak, strong or irregular. Remember always to put the past participle at the end of the sentence. The first one has been filled out as an example.

1) Ze **drinken** te veel thee. → Ze **hebben** te veel thee gedronken.

2) **Eten** jullie vlees?

____.

4) Ze **heeft** niet veel tijd.

____.

5) Het kindje **krijgt** een cadeau.

____.

6) Zien jullie die film?

____.

7) Ik **slaap** slecht.

____.

8) De film **begint**.

____.

9) Zoeken zij de bibliotheek?

____.

3) Present perfect word order. The sentences below have been scrambled. Reorder them into correct sentences in the present perfect. The first one has been filled out as an example.

1) in Denemarken / we / nog nooit / geweest / zijn
Answer: We zijn nog nooit in Denemarken geweest.

2) hun fietsen / meegebracht / hebben / ze / ?

____.

3) gegeten / hebben / geen chocolade / we

____.

4) jullie / zijn / wanneer / vertrokken / ?

____.

5) Henk / opgebeld / Carmen / heeft

____.

4) *Hebben* or ***zijn***? Complete the sentences in the present perfect below with the correct form of hebben or zijn as the auxiliary verb to go with the past participle in bold. The first one has been filled out as an example.

1) We ______zijn______ gisteren naar de nieuwe bioscoop **geweest**.

2) Zij ________________ veel **gelopen**.

3) Janneke ________________ in de vakantie heel veel boeken **gelezen**.

4) Ik ________________ uren met mijn ouders **gepraat**.

5) Onze kinderen ________________ snel **weggerend**.

6) We ________________ vorige week de leraar voor het eerst **ontmoet**.

7) ________________ je vorige week nog naar Rotterdam **geweest**?

8) Ronald ________________ helemaal naar van de stad naar huis **gelopen**.

5) Find the mistakes. There are mistakes with separable verbs in 5 of the 8 sentences below, because the separable part of the sentence in bold is in the wrong place. Find the incorrect sentences. The first one has been filled out as an example.

1) Hij wil zijn leraar niet bellen **op**.
Answer: Incorrect → Hij wil zijn leraar niet **opbellen**.

2) Mogen we deze oefening nog een keer **over**doen?

____.

3) Hebben jullie **na** erover gedacht?

____.

4) Waar moeten we **op** onze jassen hangen?

____.

5) Wie probeert het nieuwe recept vandaag **uit**?

____.

6) Elise, neem je **mee** je laptop?

____.

7) **Weg**zet je alsjeblieft die glazen?

____.

8) **Werken** Lonneke en Jan goed **samen**?

____.

8.4 WOORDENLIJST
VOCABULARY LIST

(de) acteur	actor
(de) actiefilm	action movie
(de) actrice	actress
(de) auteur	author
(de) bioscoop	cinema
(de) bloem	flower
(de) documentaire	documentary
(de) komedie	comedy
(de) leentermijn	loan term
(de) misdaadfilm	crime movie
(de) recensie	review
(de) regisseur	director
(de) rol	roll
(het) abonnement	subscription
(het) begin	beginning
(het) einde	end
(het) glas	glass
(het) kaartje	ticket
(het) lid	member
(het) lidmaatschap	membership
(het) luisterboek	audiobook
(het) pakket	package
(het) tijdschrift	magazine
(het) verhaal	story
(het) woordenboek	dictionary
aansteken	to light (a fire or cigarette)
afwassen	to wash the dishes
bijten	to bite
binnenkomen	to enter

brengen	to bring
draaien	to turn, to play a movie
dragen	to carry, to wear
dramatisch	dramatic
emotioneel	emotional
eng	scary
gelden	to be valid
geweldig	awesome
gewoon	simply
grappig	funny
hetzelfde	the same
krijgen	to receive
lenen	to lend
meebrengen	to bring along
nadenken	to think about
natuurlijk	of course
ontzettend	incredibly
opbellen	to call on the phone
ophangen	to end a phonecall
romantisch	romantic
samenwerken	to collaborate
slaan	to hit
spannend	exciting, thrilling
terugbrengen	to return
uitleggen	to explain
uitproberen	to try out
verlengen	to extend
verslaan	to defeat
weggaan	to go away
wegzetten	to put away

Tijd voor nieuwe kleren

Time for some new clothes

9
Deel
Unit

Unit 9 focuses on teaching you the colors, names of clothing items, and other vocabulary you'll need to go shopping for clothes, and practical linking words for conjunctions. You'll also learn how to conjugate comparative and superlative adjectives and how word order works in sentences with sub-clauses.

VOCABULARY	GRAMMAR
- Colors - Names of clothing items - Vocabulary to go clothes shopping - Linking words in conjunctions	- Conjugation of comparative and superlative adjectives - Word order in sub-clauses

WOORDENLIJST VOOR KLEDING (CLOTHING)				
(het) t-shirt	(de) trui	(de) broek	(de) korte broek	(de) jas
(het) overhemd	(de) jurk	(de) rok	(de) sokken	(de) schoenen
(de) stropdas	(het) badpak	(de) pyjama	(de) hoed	(de) handschoenen
(de) regenjas	(het) pak	(het) joggingpak	(de) sportschoenen	(de) laarzen

9.1 DUTCH IN CONTEXT: TIJD VOOR NIEUWE KLEREN

TIME FOR SOME NEW CLOTHES

TRACK 30 Katja and her teenage daughter Madelief go to buy new clothes for Madelief. Listen and read along with their conversation.

Katja: *Zo, Madelief, dat gele T-shirt is mooi!*

Madelief: *Dat meen je toch niet, ma? Ik ben veel te oud voor die felle kleuren!*

Katja: *Madelief, je bent zestien. Oké, ik denk dat je deze grijze rok wel mooi vindt.*

Madelief: *Een grijze rok? Wanneer ik oma ben, doe ik misschien grijze kleren aan!*

Katja: *Nou nou. Ik wist niet dat je zo kieskeurig was.*

Madelief: *Zo kieskeurig ben ik niet hoor. Kijk, die broek is wel mooi.*

Katja: *Eindelijk iets wat je mooi vindt! Welke kleur vind je mooier, felroze of bruin?*

Madelief: *Felroze natuurlijk, bruin is zo ouderwets.*

Katja: *Ik dacht dat je te oud was voor die felle kleuren?*

Madelief: *Oh ma, je begrijpt echt niks van mode hè!*

Useful phrases from the conversation:

Dat meen je toch niet, ma? → You're kidding mom, right?

Ik wist niet dat je zo kieskeurig was. → I didn't know you were that picky.

Eindelijk iets wat je mooi vindt! → Finally something you like!

Welke kleur vind je mooier, felroze of bruin? → Which color do you think is prettier, hot pink or brown?

DE KLEUREN (THE COLORS)			
Dutch	English	Dutch	English
rood	red	*roze*	pink
oranje	orange	*bruin*	brown
geel	yellow	*grijs*	gray
groen	green	*zwart*	black
blauw	blue	*wit*	white
paars	purple		

WOORDENLIJST VOOR WINKELEN (SHOPPING VOCABULARY)			
Dutch	**English**	**Dutch**	**English**
(de) kledingwinkel	clothing store	*mooi*	pretty
(de) korting	discount	*lelijk*	ugly
(de) kringloopwinkel	thrift shop	*strak*	tight
(de) kleren/kleding	clothes/clothing	*wijd*	wide
klein	small	*gaaf*	great
groot	big	*ouderwets*	old-fashioned
goedkoop	cheap	*modern*	modern
lang	long	*fel*	bright (color)
kort	short	*kieskeurig*	picky

DUTCH IN CONTEXT: VERSCHILLENDE PRIORITEITEN DIFFERENT PRIORITIES

TRACK 31 Koen and Jet are shopping for clothes. Koen likes fancy, expensive clothes, whereas Jet doesn't mind buying second-hand, and likes to spend as little as possible. Listen and read along with their conversation.

Koen: *Hey Jet, wat vind je van dit shirt? Gaaf toch? En maar veertig euro!*

Jet: *Als je het niet erg vindt om het milieu te vervuilen.*

Koen: *Wat bedoel je?*

Jet: *Kijk eens naar het etiket. Dit shirt is in Bangladesh gemaakt.*

Koen: *Nou, en? De meeste kleding wordt toch in Azië gemaakt tegenwoordig?*

Jet: *Ja, maar onder welke omstandigheden? Terwijl jij veertig euro betaalt voor dit shirt, krijgen de werknemers daar bijna niks betaald.*

Koen: *Tsja. Wat stel je dan voor?*

Jet: *Minder kleren kopen. En tweedehands kleren.*

Koen: *Oh, dat is niks voor mij.*

Jet: *Waarom niet?*

Koen: *Omdat... omdat dat raar is.*

Jet: *Waarom is dat raar?*

Koen: *Omdat die kleren dan niet meer nieuw zijn.*

Jet: *Maar zodra je dat shirt zelf hebt gedragen, is het toch ook niet meer nieuw?*

Koen: *Eigenlijk niet. Hey, laten we maar iets anders gaan doen dan samen winkelen, goed?*

Jet: *Ja, ik denk dat dat beter is!*

Useful phrases from the conversation:

Gaaf toch? → Cool, isn't it?

Als je het niet erg vindt om het milieu te vervuilen.
→ If you don't mind polluting the environment.

Terwijl jij veertig euro betaalt voor dit shirt, krijgen de werknemers daar bijna niks betaald.
→ While you're paying forty euros for this shirt, the employees there get paid next to nothing.

Wat stel je dan voor als oplossing? → What do you suggest as a solution?

Minder kleren kopen. En tweedehands kleren.
→ Buy less clothes. And second-hand clothes.

Oh, dat is niks voor mij. → Oh, that's not my thing.

Omdat dat raar is. → Because that's weird.

Maar zodra je dat shirt zelf hebt gedragen, is het toch ook niet meer nieuw?
→ But as soon as you've worn that shirt yourself, it'll no longer be new either, will it?

ONDERSCHIKKENDE VOEGWOORDEN (LINKING WORDS FOR SUB-CLAUSES)			
Dutch	English	Dutch	English
omdat	because	*of*	whether
nadat	after	*terwijl*	while
voordat	before	*zoals*	like
totdat	until	*als*	if
zodra	as soon as	*wanneer*	when
hoewel	although	*toen*	then
nu	now that		

9.2 GRAMMAR: DE VERGROTENDE EN OVERTREFFENDE TRAP VAN BIJVOEGLIJKE NAAMWOORDEN

COMPARATIVE AND SUPERLATIVE ADJECTIVES

Adjectives are very important in language, because they allow you to describe nouns. Learning how to form comparative and superlative adjectives will broaden your command of the language even further. The main grammar structures used to make adjective comparative and superlative are straightforward, but unfortunately (as always in Dutch) there are a few details to pay attention to.

Main rule for comparative and superlative adjectives.

The main rule is to add *-er* to the adjective to make it comparative, and *-st* to make it superlative. A list of regular examples is given in the table below. (Please note that we've included the translation of the comparative and the superlative for the first one, but we have omitted them for the subsequent examples for enhanced readability.)

ADJECTIVE	COMPARATIVE	SUPERLATIVE
klein (small)	*kleiner* (smaller than)	*kleinst* (smallest)
mooi (pretty)	*mooier*	*mooist*
lelijk (ugly)	*lelijker*	*lelijkst*
spannend (thrilling)	*spannender*	*spannendst*
slecht (bad)	*slechter*	*slechtst*

Example sentences with comparative and superlative adjectives:

Zijn huis is ***kleiner dan*** *mijn huis.* → His house is smaller than my house.

Deze taart is ***zoeter dan*** *die andere.* → This cake is sweeter than the other one.

Dat overhemd is ***lelijker dan*** *deze.* → That shirt is uglier than this one.

Van alle dorpen, is deze ***het mooist****.* → Out of all the villages, this one is the prettiest.

Deze film is echt ***het slechtst****.* → This movie really is the worst.

Deze scène is ***het spannendst***! → This scene is the most thrilling.*

*You can see that Dutch does not have the standard rule of using more nor most for adjectives with 2 or more syllables, but or *meest* (most) is sometimes used for the superlative if the adjective is considered very difficult to pronounce when it becomes difficult to add *-st*.

Rules for comparative adjectives only

The two rules listed below only apply to comparative adjectives.

1. **Spelling changes with open and closed syllables.** This rule is the same used when making some singular nouns plural, and in conjugating verbs. Quick recap: with open syllables that end in vowels (i.e.: *hoog, laag*) you remove one of the vowels when adding the -er, and with closed syllables with short vowels that end in consonants (i.e.: *fel, snel*) you double the consonant.

   Examples:

   strak → strak**ker**

   los → los**ser**

   groot → gr**oter**

   emotioneel → emotion**eler**

   heet → he**ter**

2. **Spelling changes to adjectives ending in -s and -f.** Add -er to adjectives that end in -f (change to v) and -s (change to z).

   Examples:

   lief → lie**ver**

   gaaf → g**aver**

   grijs → grij**zer**

   vies → vie**zer**

3. **Adjectives that end in -r.** Add *-der* to adjectives that end in *-r*.

   Examples:

   lekker → lekker**der**

   duur → duur**der**

   ver → ver**der**

   naar → naar**der**

Adding an -e to both comparative and superlative adjectives.

As we learned in Unit 5, it's often necessary to add an -e to adjectives and this rule also holds for comparative and superlative adjectives. (See Unit 5 for more details)
Have a look at the examples below:

goedkopere tas → cheaper bag

snellere auto → faster car

de duurste kaartjes → the most expensive tickets

de mooiste kleren → the most expensive clothes

Other ways to compare two things that are the same

1. **Using *even* + adjective + *als* (just as + adjective + as).**
   Mijn winkel is ***even leuk als*** *die van haar.* (My shop is just as nice as hers.)

2. **Using *net zo* + adjective + *als* (just as + adjective + as)**
   Dit boek is ***net zo spannend als*** *het vorige.* (This book is just as exciting as the previous one.)

Irregular adjectives

There's a very small group of adjectives with an irregular conjugation of the comparative and superlative. Here are the most common ones:

ADJECTIVE	COMPARATIVE	SUPERLATIVE
goed (good)	*beter* (better)	*best* (best)
veel (a lot)	*meer* (more)	*meest* (most)
weinig (little)	*minder* (less)	*minst* (least)

GRAMMAR: WOORDVOLGORDE IN BIJZINNEN WORD ORDER IN SUB-CLAUSES

In Unit 4, you already learned the basics of Dutch word order for regular sentences. We'll now dive into the world of word order with sub-clauses. The rules are clear enough, but there are several of them, so it's important to study the rules and examples detailed below and do the exercises in section 9.3.

Quick recap: a sub-clause is a part of a sentence that cannot stand on its own as a complete sentence, as it is always a compliment to the main clause of a sentence. You almost always need a specific word to link the main clause and the sub-clause, known as a subordinating conjunction.

The most common subordinating conjunction in Dutch is *dat*, which means "that". Let's compare some sentences with and without sub-clauses. We've put the subject and verb in bold, so you can see how the word order is affected, when a main clause becomes a sub-clause.

WITHOUT SUB-CLAUSE:	WITH SUB-CLAUSE:
***Ik wil** een nieuwe broek.*	*Ik denk dat **ik** een nieuwe broek **wil**.*
***Mijn sokken zijn** oud.*	*Pieter zegt dat **mijn sokken** oud **zijn**.*
***Ze hebben** oude schoenen.*	*We weten dat **ze** oude schoenen **hebben**.*
***Die jassen zijn** in de aanbieding.*	*Ze hopen dat **die jassen** in de aanbieding **zijn**.*

As you can see from these sentences in the present simple, the apparent change is that the main verb is placed at the end of the sub-clause. There are 3 more aspects to consider for word order in sub-clauses:

1. **Sentences with modal verbs and tenses with auxiliary verbs.**

   So far, you've learned the present perfect (*de voltooid tegenwoordige tijd*) and modal verbs (see Unit 7 for both), so the examples below will use those to illustrate that there are two correct ways of placing the verbs in the sub-clause.

WITHOUT SUB-CLAUSE:	WITH SUB-CLAUSE:
***Ik heb gegeten**.*	*Ik kom als **ik gegeten heb**. (or)* *Ik kom als **ik heb gegeten**.*
***Jij hebt gefietst**.*	*Hij vroeg wanneer **jij hebt gefietst**. (or)* *Hij vroeg wanneer **jij gefietst hebt**.*
***De verkopers moeten** goed **uitleggen**.*	*Zij vindt dat **de verkopers** goed **moeten uitleggen** (or)* *Zij vindt dat **de verkopers** goed **uit moeten leggen**.*

2. **Separable verbs.**

In Unit 8, you learned that there are a lot of separable verbs in Dutch, meaning that in the present simple tense the separable part comes separately at the end of the sentence. However, in sub-clauses, they reunite and have to be placed at the end of the sentence.

WITHOUT SUB-CLAUSE:	WITH SUB-CLAUSE:
Ze werken samen.	*Ik geloof dat* ***ze samenwerken***.
Jij wast af.	*We gaan als* ***jij afwast***.
Hoe laat ***gaan de gasten weg***?	*Hoe laat denk je dat* ***de gasten weggaan***?
De student denkt na.	*We wachten terwijl* ***de student nadenkt***.

3. **Word order when the sub-clause comes first.**

In all the examples above, we've started the sentence with the main clause, followed by the sub-clause. However, in many cases, we start the sentence with a sub-clause, followed by the main clause. When you do this in Dutch, the main verb of the main clause needs to come first.

We gaan 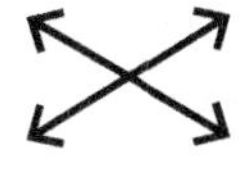 ***als jij afwast.*** (Main clause: *we gaan* / sub-clause: *als jij afwast*)

Als jij afwast ***gaan we.***

More examples:

MAIN CLAUSE FIRST:	SUB-CLAUSE FIRST:
Ik help met schoonmaken als ze het goed vindt.	Als ze het goed vindt, ***help ik*** met schoonmaken.
We kopen een groter huis nadat we de loterij hebben gewonnen.	Nadat we de loterij hebben gewonnen, ***kopen we*** een groter huis.
Hij voelt zich beter wanneer hij terug is van de doktersafspraak.	Wanneer hij terug is van de doktersafspraak, ***voelt hij*** zich beter.
Je moet je huidige huis verkopen voordat je dat huis koopt.	Voordat je dat huis koopt, ***moet je*** je huidige huis verkopen.
De vogels worden wakker nadat de zon opkomt.	Nadat de zon opkomt, ***worden de vogels*** wakker.
Je krijgt misschien promotie als je hard genoeg werkt.	Als je hard genoeg werkt, ***krijg je*** misschien promotie.

9.3 OEFENINGEN
EXERCISES

1) Names of items of clothing. Describe the item of clothing that appears in the left column, including the color. Plural nouns do not need the article *een*. The first one has been filled out as an example.

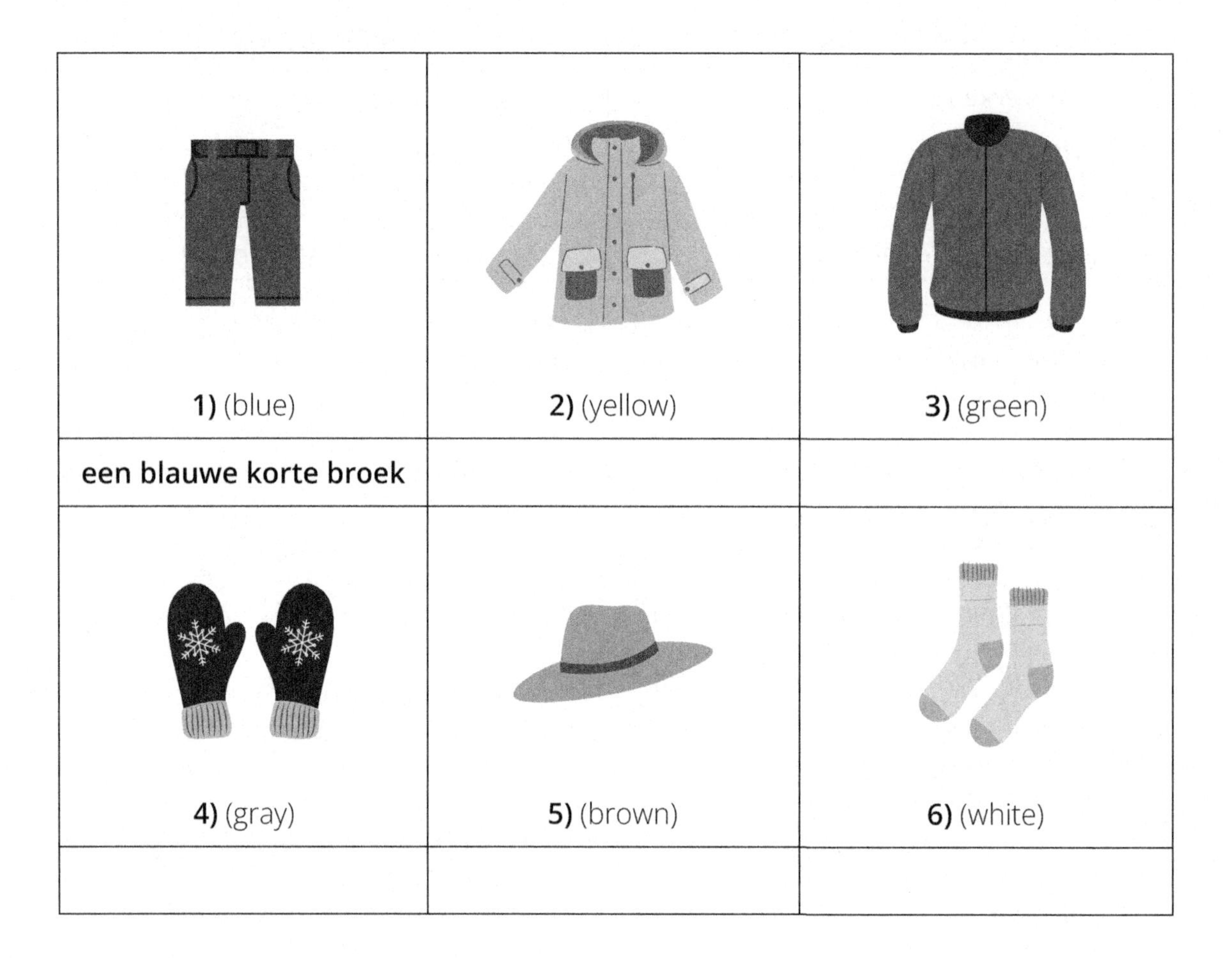

1) (blue)	**2)** (yellow)	**3)** (green)
een blauwe korte broek		
4) (gray)	**5)** (brown)	**6)** (white)

2) Comparative adjectives. Write sentences about the images using the comparative form of the adjective provided. The first one has been filled out as an example.

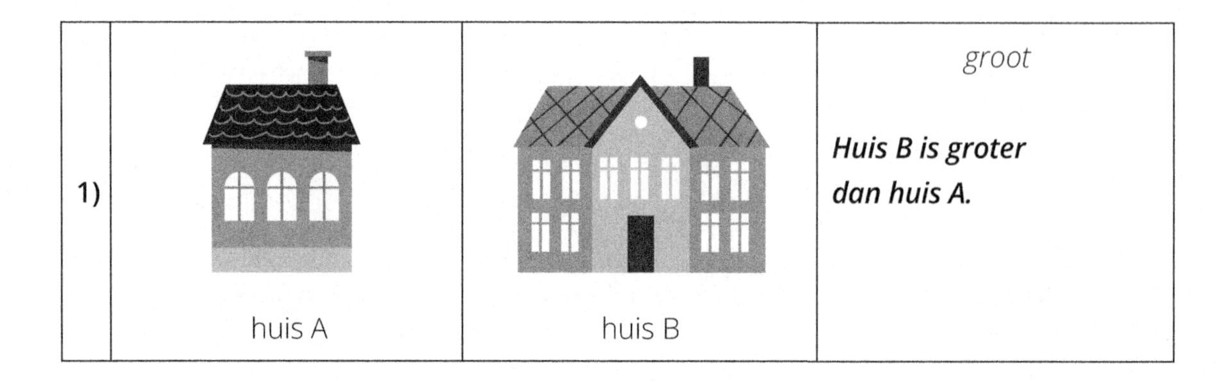

1)	huis A	huis B	*groot* ***Huis B is groter dan huis A.***

2)	 jurk 1	 jurk 2	mooi
3)	 tas A	 tas B	donker
4)	 schoenen 1	 schoenen 2	oud
5)	 tafel 1	 tafel 2	schoon
6)	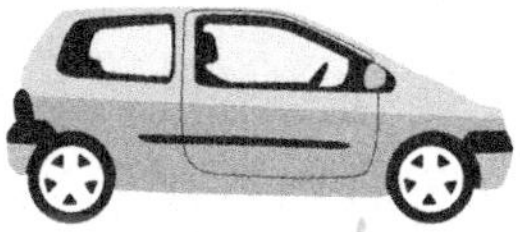 auto A	 auto B	duur

3) Superlative adjectives. The table below contains data on different topics. Write sentences about the given information by using the comparative form of the adjective provided. The first one has been filled out as an example.

1)	**Gemiddeld maandelijks inkomen per land** 1) Ierland: $ 5.468 2) Polen: $ 1.270 3) Frankrijk: $ 3.290	hoog **Het inkomen in Ierland is het hoogst.**
2)	**Gemiddelde diepte van oceanen en zeeën** 1) De Beringzee: 1.640 meter diep 2) De Grote Oceaan: 4.280 meter diep 3) De Indische Oceaan: 3.741 meter diep	diep
3)	**Oppervlakte van landen** 1) Rusland: 17.098/242 km^2 2) Griekenland: 131/990 km^2 3) Brazilië: 8.515.770 km^2	klein
4)	**Snelheid van de bevolkingsgroei 2011-2020** 1) Egypte: 2,31% 2) Zuid Afrika: 1,48% 3) Japan: -0,18%	snel
5)	**Geboortedatums van bekende zangeressen** 1) Norah Jones: 30 maart 1979 2) Lady Gaga: 28 maart 1986 3) Madonna: 16 augustus 1958	oud
6)	**Prijs van bekende schilderijen** 1) De Vaandeldrager van Rembrandt van Rijn: $213.000.000 2) Zelfportret zonder baard van Vincent van Gogh: $71/500.000 3) Interchanged van Willem de Kooning: $300.000/000	duur

4) Main clauses and sub-clauses. Below you'll see sentences with only a main clause. Rewrite the sentence with a new main clause, changing the old main clause into a sub-clause. The first one has been filled out as an example.

1) Die broek is lelijk. (Ik vind dat) → Ik vind dat die broek lelijk is.

2) We gaan niet naar de bioscoop. (Mijn moeder zegt dat)

____.

3) Dat boek is echt saai. (Mijn vriendin vindt dat)

____.

4) Tieners willen veel reizen. (In het boek staat dat)

____.

5) Marjolein zingt heel mooi. (Haar ouders zeggen dat)

____.

6) Je mag niet roken in het vliegtuig. (In de regels staat dat)

____.

7) De studenten vragen veel. (De leraar vindt dat)

____.

8) Het kindje huilt hard. (De buren vinden dat)

____.

5) Main clauses and sub-clauses. Match the main clauses with their sub-clauses. The first one has been filled out as an example.

F	**1)** Wanneer je veel leest,	**a)** zal ze nog een paar keer vallen.
	2) Als je naar de winkel gaat,	**b)** willen sommige organisaties het nu verbieden.
	3) Nadat onze reis over was,	**c)** kan je al goed Nederlands spreken.
	4) Toen de dramatische film was afgelopen,	**d)** kan je dan voor mij bananen kopen?
	5) Omdat mensen te veel plastic gebruiken,	**e)** waren veel mensen in de bioscoop emotioneel.
	6) Totdat het kindje goed leert fietsen,	**f)** zal je veel nieuwe woorden leren.
	7) Voordat je het weet,	**g)** misten we het strand heel erg.

9.4 WOORDENLIJST
VOCABULARY LIST

(de) aanbieding	discounted price
(de) bevolkingsgroei	population growth
(de) broek	pants
(de) diepte	depth
(de) geboortedatum	birth date
(de) handschoenen	gloves
(de) jas	coat
(de) jurk	dress
(de) kleding	clothing
(de) kledingwinkel	clothing store
(de) kleren	clothes
(de) kleur	color
(de) korte broek	shorts
(de) kringloopwinkel	thrift shop
(de) laarzen	boots
(de) omstandigheden	circumstances
(de) oppervlakte	surface area
(het) pak	suit
(de) pyjama	pajamas
(de) regenjas	raincoat
(de) schoenen	shoes
(de) snelheid	speed
(de) sok	sock
(de) sportschoenen	sports shoes
(de) stropdas	tie
(de) tas	bag
(de) trui	sweater
(de) werknemer	employee
(het) inkomen	income

(het) joggingpak	jogging suit
(het) overhemd	shirt
(het) badpak	swimsuit
als	if
bekend	(well-)known
blauw	blue
bruin	brown
donker	dark
fel	bright (color)
gaaf	great
geel	yellow
groen	green
groot	big
hard	hard, loudly
hoewel	although
kieskeurig	picky
klein	small
kort	short
lelijk	ugly
maandelijks	monthly
menen	to mean
modern	modern
naar	to
nadat	after
nu	now
of	or
omdat	because
oranje	orange (color)
ouderwets	old-fashioned
paars	purple
raar	weird
roken	to smoke

roze	pink
strak	tight
terwijl	while
toen	then
totdat	until
voordat	before
wijd	wide
zoals	as soon as
zodra	as soon as
zwart	black

Het huis van mijn dromen

My dream home

10
Deel
Unit

Unit 10 focuses on teaching you the vocabulary to describe homes, including the different rooms and parts of the home, and the furniture in it. You'll also learn how to talk about the future with three different Dutch grammar constructions, and you learn to form diminutives.

VOCABULARY	GRAMMAR
- Parts of the home - Furniture	- How to talk about the future - Forming diminutives

10.1 DUTCH IN CONTEXT: HET HUIS VAN MIJN DROMEN

MY DREAM HOME

TRACK 32 Karel is about to move to a new house, which is his absolute dream home. He randomly runs into his friend Robbie and tells him all about it. Listen and read along with their conversation.

Karel: *Robbie! Hey, dat is lang geleden!*

Robbie: *Hey Karel! Hoe is het?*

Karel: *Goed! Woon je nog steeds hier in de buurt?*

Robbie: *Nee, ik ben vorig jaar verhuisd. En jij?*

Karel: *Ik woon hier nog wel, maar over drie dagen verhuizen we!*

Robbie: *Oh, waarheen?*

Karel: *Naar het huis van mijn dromen, in Wassenaar.*

Robbie: *Tjonge jonge!! Gefeliciteerd!*

Karel: *Ja, het is echt prachtig. Suzanne zal het inrichten. We gaan dus wel wat nieuwe meubels kopen.*

Robbie: *En wat gaan jullie dan met jullie huidige meubels doen?*

Karel: *Die zullen we verkopen, denk ik.*

Robbie: *Ik heb nog wat meubels nodig...*

Karel: *Aha! Geef je telefoonnummer maar! Dan zal ik je laten weten welke meubels we gaan verkopen!*

Robbie: *Top!*

Useful phrases from the conversation:

Hey, dat is lang geleden! → Hey, it's been so long!

Woon je nog steeds hier in de buurt? → Do you still live around here?

Oh, waarheen? → Oh, where to?

Naar het huis van mijn dromen. → To my dream home.

Gefeliciteerd! → Congratulations!

Suzanne zal het inrichten. → Suzanne will decorate it.

En wat gaan jullie dan met jullie huidige meubels doen? → And what are you going to do with the furniture you currently have?

Die zullen we verkopen, denk ik. → We'll sell them, I think.

MEUBELS (FURNITURE)				
(het) bed	*(de) tafel*	*(de) bank*	*(de) klerenkast*	*(het) gordijn*
(de) boekenkast	*(de) fauteuil*	*(het) bureau*	*(de) stoel*	*(de) lamp*
(de) wasmachine	*(de) afwasmachine*	*(de) magnetron*	*(de) kussens*	*(de) spiegel*

In the table below, you'll see pictures of the different rooms in a home and a description of the furniture and home appliances in each room.

KAMERS IN EEN HUIS (ROOMS IN A HOME)			
De keuken **(kitchen)**	Er is een fornuis, oven, koelkast, magnetron, wasbak en er zijn keukenkastjes.	***De slaapkamer*** **(bedroom)**	Er staan een bed en een tafel. Er hangen een schilderij en een boekenplank aan de muur.
De eetkamer **(dining room)**	Er staat een tafel met twee stoelen en er hangen twee lampen aan het plafond. Er zijn ook vier ramen.	***De badkamer*** **(bathroom)**	Er is een bad, een kast en aan de muur hangen een handdoek en een badjas.
De huiskamer **(livingroom)**	Er is een fauteuil, een klein tafeltje, en aan de muur hangen twee planken en een schilderij.	***De studeerkamer*** **(study)**	Er is een boekenkast, een bureau met een bureaustoel en aan de muur hangt een klok.

10.2 GRAMMAR: OVER DE TOEKOMST PRATEN

TALKING ABOUT THE FUTURE

Finally, a grammar topic that's pretty straightforward: how to talk about the future. There are three ways of talking about future events, and they're all pretty simple!

1. **Using the present simple (*onvoltooid tegenwoordige tijd*)**

   In Unit 2, you learned how to conjugate the present simple, and we'd already explained how this tense is also very often used to talk about the future. (In the examples below, we've decided to use the present continuous in the English translation, but it could also be translated using will + verb.)

   Ik eet morgen bij mijn vriend. → I'm having dinner at my (boy)friend's tomorrow.

   Ze speelt vrijdag een wedstrijd. → She's playing a match on Friday.

   We verhuizen volgende week. → We're moving next week.

   Ze maken vanavond het huis schoon. → They're cleaning the house tonight.

2. **Using the verb *gaan* (to go)**

   This construction of using the verb gaan (to go) + infinitive verb is quite similar to the English construction of going to + infinitive verb.

   Je gaat volgend jaar verhuizen. → You're going to move next year.

   Wanneer gaat hij zijn boek publiceren? → When is he going to publish his book?

   De eenden gaan zwemmen. → The ducks are going to swim.

   Het gaat gelukkig niet regenen. → Fortunately, it's not going to rain.

3. **Using the verb *zullen (onvoltooid tegenwoordige toekomende tijd)***

   Finally, the third and last way of talking about the future is a construction of the auxiliary verb *zullen* (will/shall) + infinitive verb.

PERSONAL PRONOUN	ZULLEN (AUXILIARY VERB)	VERBS IN THE INFINITIVE	ENGLISH TRANSLATION
ik	*zal*	*verhuizen*	*I will move*
je, u	*zult/zal**	*kopen*	*you will buy*
hij, ze, het	*zal*	*helpen*	*he, she, it will help*
we	*zullen*	*opruimen*	*we will tidy up*
jullie	*zullen*	*vragen*	*you will ask*
u	*zult*	*denken*	*you will think*
ze	*zullen*	*schoonmaken*	*they will clean*

*You can see that there are two options here for the second person singular, *zult* and *zal*. Both can be used for the informal *je* and the formal *u*, and both are correct. The difference lies in how formal they sound. Most people will prefer *u zult* over *u zal*, and *je zal* over *je zult*.

GRAMMAR: VERKLEINWOORDEN DIMINUTIVES

Diminutives are used a lot in Dutch. They do not only show that something is actually physically small, but are also used to convey a sense of affection. The basic rule is to add *-je* to the noun, so let's look at some examples before we take you through the exceptions to that rule.

het huis → het huis***je***

de wolk → het wolk***je***

de bank → het bank***je***

de broek → het broek***je***

de fiets → het fiets***je***

Please note that all diminutives take the article *het* in singular (*het fietsje*) but take *de* as do all plurals (*de fietsjes*).

Now, let's have a look at the exceptions to the basic rule.

1. -***tje*** is added in the following cases:

   a. To nouns ending in a vowel (and a, o and u are doubled)

      auto → autoo***tje***

      oma → omaa***tje***

   b. To nouns with diphthongs

      touw → touw***tje***

      ei → ei***tje***

   c. nouns ending in -l, -n and -r that are preceded by a long vowel, diphthong or a weak vowel

      stoel → stoel***tje*** (oe: diphthong)

      maan → maan***tje*** (aa: long vowel)

      kamer → kamer***tje*** (-er: weak vowel)

   d. 'tje is added to nouns ending in y

      baby → baby'***tje***

2. ***-etje*** is added to nouns ending in -l, -m, -n, -r, or –ng, where the consonant is doubled, except for words ending in -ng.

      ster → sterr***etje***

      zon → zonn***etje***

      stem → stemm***etje***

      ding → ding***etje***

3. ***-pje*** is added in the following cases:

   a. nouns ending in -m preceded by a long vowel

      raam → raam***pje***

      probleem → probleem***pje***

b. nouns ending in -m preceded by a weak vowel

bodem → bodem***pje***

c. nouns ending in -m preceded by a diphthong

duim → duim***pje***

bloem → bloem***pje***

d. nouns ending in -m preceded by r or l:

arm → arm***pje***

helm → helm***pje***

4. ***-kje*** is added to nouns ending in -ing if the penultimate syllable is stressed. The -g must be removed too so you're left with -inkje.

pudding → pudd***inkje***

ketting → kett***inkje***

Please note that some words that seem like a simple diminutive actually take on a whole new meaning:

het brood (bread) → *het broodje* (breadroll)

de telefoon (telephone) → *telefoontje* (telephone call)

de kaart (map or postcard) → *kaartje* (entrance ticket)

het riet (reed) → het *rietje* (drinking straw)

And there are also a few words that only exist as diminutives:

meisje → girl (the word *meid* does exist, but is not the standard term)

poffertje → tiny pancake served with powdered sugar

toetje → dessert

sprookje → fairytale

Pronunciation note

TRACK 33 Lastly, it's important to pay attention to the pronunciation, especially of diminutives ending in *-tje*, *-dje* and *-sje*.

1. ***-tje and -dje.*** The e in the diminutive is never stressed, and is therefore pronounced as the schwa sound in English. The combination of the t and j in ***-tje*** make a ch-sound. The International Phonetic Alphabet reference would be ['ʧə'].

   Listen to the recording of the words below and repeat them:

   omaatje

   kindje

   kamertje

2. ***-sje.*** Again, the e takes on a schwa sound, but the combination of the s and j in -sje make a sh-sound. The International Phonetic Alphabet reference would be ['ʃə'].

   Listen to the recording of the words below and repeat them:

   meisje

   huisje

   glaasje

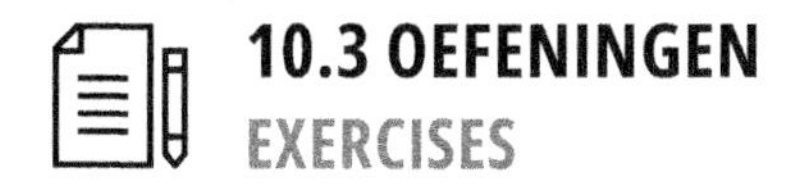

10.3 OEFENINGEN
EXERCISES

1) Match the descriptions of the rooms with the pictures. Pay close attention, because the descriptions also use negatives. The first one has been filled out as an example.

	Pictures of rooms	Descriptions of the furniture in the rooms
1)		**a)** In deze kamer zie je een tafel met bloemen, stoelen en vier ramen. Er is geen bed en ook geen boekenkast. Description of picture: **4, de eetkamer**
2)		**b)** In deze kamer zie je een bed, een klein tafeltje, een boekenplank, een schilderij en een raam. Er zijn geen tafels en geen open haard. Description of picture: ______________________
3)		**c)** In deze kamer zie je een koelkast, keukenkastjes, en een fornuis. Er zijn geen tafels of stoelen. Description of picture: ______________________
4)		**d)** In deze kamer zie je een boekenkast, een bureau met een lamp en een computer erop, en een stoel. Aan de muur hangt een klok en er is een raam. Er is geen televisie of bed. Description of picture: ______________________
5)		**e)** In deze kamer zie je een fauteuil, een schilderij en twee boekenplankjes. Er zijn geen ramen of deuren. Description of picture: ______________________

6)		**f)** In deze kamer zie je een badkuip, kast en een raam. Er is geen koelkast of fornuis. Description of picture: ___________

2) Create the diminutive. The first one has been filled out as an example.

1) buik ______**buikje**______.

2) hart ____________________.

3) bril ____________________.

4) dokter ____________________.

5) mama ____________________.

6) minuut ____________________.

7) bal ____________________.

8) boerderij ____________________.

9) man ____________________.

10) leerling ____________________.

3) Write a future sentence with the subject and verb given, also using the verb *gaan*. The first one has been filled out as an example.

1) We / geschiedenis studeren ______**We gaan geschiedenis studeren.**______.

2) Jullie / een pizza bakken / ? ____________________.

3) Ik / niet douchen ____________________.

4) Jouw ouders / lekker koken ____________________.

5) Je / een boek schrijven / ? ____________________.

6) Henk / zijn huis verven ____________________.

4) Write a future sentence with the subject and verb given, also using the verb *zullen*.
The first one has been filled out as an example.

1) De dokters / een moeilijke operatie / uitvoeren

De dokters zullen een moeilijke operatie uitvoeren.

2) Jouw moeder / niet boos worden

____.

3) Johanna en Paul / helpen met koken

____.

4) Jullie / vanavond op tijd zijn / ?

____.

5) Onze kleren / nat worden

____.

6) U / geen korting krijgen

____.

5) Read the text below about Karin who is telling the man from the moving company where to put the furniture in her new house, then answer the questions.
Be careful because she changes her instructions a lot, always use the last one. The first one has been filled out as an example.

Oké Piet, zet die bank in de huiskamer en de stoelen in de keuken. Die tafel moet boven in de studeerkamer. Die grote dozen mag je in de slaapkamer neerzetten en het bed ook. De klok en die lampen moeten naar de huiskamer. En zet je de wasmachine in de badkamer? O nee, zet maar in de keuken. Weet je, zet de stoelen ook maar in de huiskamer!

1) Waar staat de wasmachine?

De wasmachine staat in de keuken.

2) Waar staan de stoelen?

____.

3) Waar staan de grote dozen en het bed?

____.

4) Waar staat de bank?

____.

10.4 WOORDENLIJST
VOCABULARY LIST

(de) afwasmachine	dishwasher
(de) badjas	bathrobe
(de) badkamer	bathroom
(de) badkuip	bathtub
(de) bodem	bottom (floor)
(de) boekenkast	bookcase
(de) bureaustoel	desk chair
(de) buurt	neighborhood, vicinity
(de) duim	thumb
(de) eetkamer	dining room
(de) fauteuil	armchair
(de) helm	helmet
(de) huiskamer	living room
(de) kamer	room
(de) keuken	kitchen
(de) keukenkastjes	kitchen cabinets
(de) klerenkast	wardrobe
(de) kussens	pillows, cushions
(de) lamp	lamp
(de) magnetron	microwave
(de) meubels	furniture
(de) open haard	fireplace
(de) slaapkamer	bedroom
(de) spiegel	mirror
(de) ster	star, celebrity
(de) stoel	chair
(de) studeerkamer	study
(de) tafel	table
(de) wasbak	sink

(de) wasmachine	washing machine
(de) wedstrijd	match, game
(het) bed	bed
(het) bureau	desk
(het) fornuis	stove
(het) gordijn	curtain
(het) plafond	ceiling
(het) raam	window
(het) schilderij	painting
(het) touw	rope
gefeliciteerd	congratulations
huidig	current
inrichten	to decorate
opruimen	to tidy
publiceren	to publish
top	excellent
verhuizen	to move
waarheen	where to

ANTWOORDEN OP DE OEFENINGEN
ANSWER KEY

UNIT 1

Unit 1 - Exercise 7

2) B: oog
3) B: duur
4) C: pijn
5) B: bus
6) A: doen
7) C: lauw
8) A: tien

Unit 1 - Exercise 8

2) nicht
3) zus
4) dochter
5) man
6) oma
7) broer
8) opa
9) moeder
10) oom
11) tante

UNIT 2

Unit 2 - Exercise 1

2) Ik heet Marc Smith. Ik kom uit Groot-Brittannië. Ik ben ingenieur.
3) Mijn naam is Johann Schmitt. Ik kom uit Duitsland. Ik ben politicus.
4) Ik ben Yanet Sanchez. Ik kom uit Spanje. Ik ben lerares.

Unit 2 - Exercise 2

2) kom
3) is
4) hebben
5) heet
6) vragen
7) komen
8) zijn
9) bent

Unit 2 - Exercise 3

1) werken
2) heet
3) komt
4) lopen
5) vraagt
6) zijn
7) heet
8) ben

Unit 2 - Exercise 4

2) De
3) De
4) Het
5) De

UNIT 3

Unit 3 - Exercise 1

2) Aan de linkerkant is **de universiteit**.
3) Aan de rechterkant van de hoofdstraat, naast de apotheek is **het ziekenhuis**.
4) Tegenover de bibliotheek is **het kantoor**.

Unit 3 - Exercise 2

2) Heet jij Armando?
3) Lopen de toeristen op het plein?
4) Neemt zij de bus?
5) Zijn jullie in de apotheek?
6) Hebben zij een schoenenwinkel?
7) Fietsen de kinderen naar school?
8) Zoek je het restaurant?

Unit 3 - Exercise 3

2) Hoeveel
3) Welk
4) Wat
5) Wie
6) Waar
7) Wanneer

Unit 3 - Exercise 4

2) Apotheken
3) Ziekenhuizen
4) Chefs
5) Beroepen
6) Trams
7) Restaurants
8) Vliegvelden
9) Auto's
10) Scholen

Unit 3 - Exercise 5

2) Er is
3) Er zijn
4) Er zijn
5) Er zijn
6) Er zijn
7) Er is
8) Er zijn

Unit 3 - Exercise 6:

2) Is er
3) Zijn er
4) Zijn er
5) Zijn er
6) Zijn er
7) Is er
8) Zijn er

UNIT 4

Unit 4 - Exercise 1

2) Hoeveel kosten de rode bieten? → €0.89/ negenentachtig cent per kilo.
3) Hoeveel kosten de wortels? → €2.99 / twee euro negenennegentig per kilo.
4) Hoeveel kosten de uien? → €0.70 / zeventig cent per kilo.
5) Hoeveel kost de sla? → €1 / één euro per stuk.
6) Hoeveel kost de komkommer? → €0.89 / negenentachtig cent per stuk.

Unit 4 - Exercise 2

93 - drieënnegentig
38 - achtendertig
44 - vierenveertig
214 - tweehonderdveertien
167 - honderzevenenzestig
555 - vijfhonderdvijfenvijftig
771 - zevenhonderdeenenzeventig
1234 - eenduizend tweehonderdvierendertig
3411 - drieduizend vierhonderdelf
6856 - zesduizend achthonderdzesenvijftig
2018 - tweeduizend achttien

Unit 4 - Exercise 3

2) dit
3) die
4) deze
5) die
6) deze
7) Die
8) deze

Unit 4 - Exercise 4

2) We verkopen geen computers.
3) De kinderen willen niet schoonmaken.
4) Georgina houdt niet van kersen.
5) De auto's staan niet goed geparkeerd.
6) Mijn vrienden spreken geen Engels.
7) De druiven zijn niet duur.
8) Er is geen supermarkt.

Unit 4 - Exercise 5

2) We lopen vanavond snel naar huis. / or / Vanavond lopen we snel naar huis.
3) Jullie willen om 4 uur meteen naar het vliegveld. / or / Om 4 uur willen jullie meteen naar het vliegveld.
4) De dieren rennen altijd snel naar buiten. / or / Altijd rennen de dieren snel naar buiten.
5) De student koopt morgen goedkoop fruit op de markt. / or / Morgen koopt de student goedkoop fruit op de markt.
6) Die dokters en verpleegsters werken iedere dag in het ziekenhuis. / or / Iedere dag werken die dokters en verpleegsters in het ziekenhuis.

UNIT 5

Unit 5 - Exercise 1

2) 10:15 – Het is kwart over tien.
3) 11:20 – Het is tien voor half twaalf. / Het is twintig over elf.
4) 02:30 – Het is half drie.
5) 04:35 – Het is vijf over half vijf.
6) 06:45 – Het is kwart voor zeven.
7) 07:55 – Het is vijf voor acht.
8) 09:00 – Het is negen uur.

Unit 5 - Exercise 2

2) Op dinsdag gaat hij om 6 uur **werken**.
3) Op woensdag gaat hij 's avonds naar de **schaakclub**.
4) Op donderdag is hij om 3 uur op de **universiteit**.
5) Op vrijdag gaat hij om **11** uur naar de universiteit.
6) Op zaterdag gaat hij 's avonds om **6** uur **werken**.
7) Op zondagmiddag gaat hij **voetballen**.

Unit 5 - Exercise 4

2) Op woensdag wordt de maximale temperatuur 18 graden.
3) Op donderdag wordt het zonnig.
4) Op vrijdag wordt het 25 graden.
5) Op woensdag waait het.
6) Op zaterdag wordt de maximale temperatuur 16 graden.
7) Op zaterdag regent het.

Unit 5 - Exercise 5

2) mij
3) Ze
4) Wij
5) hem
6) hen
7) hem
8) Het
9) ze

Unit 5 - Exercise 6

2) Jullie schrijven **hem.**
3) Wij sturen een e-mail naar **hen.**
4) Heeft u vragen voor **ons.**
5) Ze helpen **hem.**
6) We gaan **haar** ophalen.
7) Ze liggen op tafel.

Unit 5 - Exercise 7

2) lekker
3) koele
4) lief
5) grijze
6) oranje
7) mooie
8) heerlijke
9) pittige
10) houten

Unit 5 - Exercise 8

2) dure
3) mistige
4) warm
5) lekkere
6) zoet
7) hete
8) goedkoop

UNIT 6

Unit 6 - Exercise 1

2) het bot
3) de mond
4) de gezichten
5) de arm
6) de hand
7) de voet
8) de schouder
9) de benen
10) het haar
11) de rug
12) het oor
13) de neus
14) de longen
15) het hart
16) de teen

Unit 6 - Exercise 2

2) last
3) zwanger
4) klachten
5) maanden
6) pijn
7) medicijnen
8) zorgen

Unit 6 - Exercise 3

2) ons
3) je
4) ons
5) zich
6) me
7) zich
8) je

Unit 6 - Exercise 4

2) onze
3) haar
4) mijn
5) jouw
6) jullie
7) ons
8) hun
9) zijn
10) uw

Unit 6 - Exercise 5

English translation	Adding an *s*	Possessive adjective	Using *van* (of)
1) Mother's knee	*Moeders knie*	*Haar knie*	*De knie van moeder*
2) Hanneke's neighbors (f)	*Hannekes buren*	*Haar buren*	*De buren van Hanneke*
3) Ahmed's heart	*Ahmeds hart*	*Zijn hart*	*Het hart van Ahmed*
4) Jan's farm (m)	*Jans boerderij*	*Zijn boerderij*	*De boerderij van Jan*
5) Petra and Karel's car	*Petra en Karels auto*	*Hun auto*	*De auto van Petra en Karel*
6) Piet and my GP	*(not possible)*	*Onze huisarts*	*De huisarts van Piet en mij*
7) My sister's phone	*(not possible)*	*Haar telefoon*	*De telefoon van mijn zus*

Unit 6 - Exercise 6

2) De verpleegster is de wond aan het verbinden.
3) Is de hond zich aan het krabben?
4) Ik ben geen avondeten aan het koken.
5) Is Anna aan het studeren?
6) Jij en Klaas zijn naar de bushalte aan het rennen.
7) De chauffeur is zich aan het haasten.
8) De tieners zijn niet aan het opletten.

UNIT 7

Unit 7 - Exercise 1

2) bestemming
3) vertraging
4) inchecken
5) riem
6) koffer
7) vertrekken
8) toilet

Unit 7 - Exercise 2

1) het strand
2) de heuvel
3) het meer
4) de woestijn
5) de waterval
6) de rivier
7) de zee
8) de berg
9) de vallei
10) het eiland
11) het bos
12) de kust

Unit 7 - Exercise 3

2) f
3) a
4) c
5) b
6) g
7) h
8) e

Unit 7 - Exercise 4

2) mag
3) kunnen
4) moet
5) kan
6) Mag
7) willen
8) kunnen
9) moeten / mogen
10) wil

Unit 7 - Exercise 5

2) Ik heb het excuus niet geloofd.
3) Is Klaartje naar Azië gereisd?
4) Het heeft de hele nacht geregend.
5) Mijn zus heeft veel gelezen.
6) Heeft u gisteren gedanst?
7) De brandweer heeft de hond gered.
8) De ouders hebben niet naar de directrice geluisterd.
9) Het meisje heeft de tekening gekleurd.
10) Heb jij ons gemaild?

Unit 7 - Exercise 6

2) gemist
3) gewerkt
4) gevraagd
5) gedeeld
6) geleefd
7) gezet
8) geverfd
9) gelegd
10) geleerd

UNIT 8

Unit 8 - Exercise 1

2) grappig
3) auteurs
4) Laten
5) eng
6) kaartjes
7) terugbrengen
8) begin
9) lid
10) recensie

Unit 8 - Exercise 2

2) Mijn zusje heeft de boeken naar de bibliotheek gebracht.
3) Hebben jullie vlees gegeten?
4) Jouw ouders zijn vaak gekomen.
5) Ze heeft niet veel tijd gehad.
6) Het kindje heeft een cadeau gekregen.
7) Hebben jullie die film gezien?
8) Ik heb slecht geslapen.
9) De film is begonnen.
10) Hebben zij de bibliotheek gezocht?

Unit 8 - Exercise 3

2) Hebben ze hun fietsen meegebracht?
3) We hebben geen chocolade gegeten.
4) Wanneer zijn jullie vertrokken?
5) Henk heeft Carmen opgebeld.
6) Het feest is nog niet begonnen
7) Heeft u de sleutels al gevonden?
8) Mark heeft me net geschreven.

Unit 8 - Exercise 4

2) hebben
3) heeft
4) heb
5) zijn
6) hebben
7) Ben
8) is

Unit 8 - Exercise 5

2) Correct
3) Incorrect: Hebben jullie erover **nagedacht**?
4) Incorrect: Waar moeten we onze jassen **ophangen**?
5) Correct
6) Incorrect: Elise, neem je je laptop **mee**?
7) Incorrect: Zet je alsjeblieft die glazen **weg**?
8) Correct

UNIT 9

Unit 9 - Exercise 1

2) een gele jas
3) een groene trui
4) grijze handschoenen
5) een bruine hoed
6) witte sokken

Unit 9 - Exercise 2

2) Jurk 1 is mooier dan jurk 2
3) Tas B is donkerder dan tas A.
4) Schoenen 2 zijn ouder dan schoenen 1.
5) Tafel 1 is schoner dan tafel 2.
6) Auto B is duurder dan auto A.

Unit 9 - Exercise 3

2) De Grote Oceaan is het diepst.
3) Griekenland is het kleinst.
4) De bevolkingsgroei van Egypte is het snelst.
5) Madonna is het oudst.
6) Interchanged van Willem de Kooning is het duurst.

Unit 9 - Exercise 4

2) Mijn moeder zegt dat we niet naar de bioscoop gaan.
3) Mijn vriendin vindt dat dat boek echt saai is.
4) In het boek staat dat tieners veel willen reizen.
5) Haar ouders zeggen dat Marjolein heel mooi zingt.
6) In de regels staat dat je niet mag roken in het vliegtuig.
7) De leraar vindt dat de studenten veel vragen.
8) De buren vinden dat het kindje hard huilt.

Unit 9 - Exercise 5

2) d – Als je naar de winkel gaat, kan je dan voor mij bananen kopen?
3) g – Nadat onze reis over was, misten we het strand heel erg.
4) e – Toen de dramatische film was afgelopen, waren veel mensen in de bioscoop emotioneel.
5) b – Omdat mensen te veel plastic gebruiken, willens sommige organisaties het nu verbieden.
6) a – Totdat het kindje goed leert fietsen, zal ze nog een paar keer vallen.
7) c – Voordat je het weet, kan je al goed Nederlands spreken.

UNIT 10

Unit 10 - Exercise 1

2) 5, de slaapkamer
3) 2, de keuken
4) 1, de studeerkamer
5) 6, de huiskamer
6) 3, de badkamer

Unit 10 - Exercise 2

2) hartje
3) brilletje
4) doktertje
5) mamaatje
6) minuutje
7) balletje
8) boerderijtje
9) mannetje
10) leerlingetje

Unit 10 - Exercise 3

2) Gaan jullie een pizza bakken?
3) Ik ga niet douchen.
4) Jouw ouders gaan lekker koken.
5) Ga je een boek schrijven?
6) Henk gaat zijn huis verven.

Unit 10 - Exercise 4

2) Jouw moeder zal niet boos worden.
3) Johanna en Paul zullen helpen met koken.
4) Zullen jullie vanavond op tijd zijn?
5) Onze kleren zullen nat worden.
6) U zal/zult geen korting krijgen. (Both *zal* and *zult* are correct)

Unit 10 - Exercise 5

2) The stoelen staan in de huiskamer.
3) De grote dozen en het bed staan in de slaapkamer.
4) De bank staat in de huiskamer.

COMPLETE WOORDENLIJST
COMPLETE VOCABULARY LIST

(de) aanbieding	special offer
(de) aankomsthal	arrival hall
(de) aardappel	potato
(de) aardbei	strawberry
(de) accountant	accountant
(de) acteur	actor
(de) actiefilm	action movie
(de) actrice	actress
(de) advocaat	lawyer
(de) afspraak	appointment, agreement
(de) afwasmachine	dishwasher
(de) allergie	allergy
(de) apotheek	pharmacy
(de) appel	apple
(de) architect	architect
(de) arm	arm
(de) asperge	asparagus
(de) auteur	author
(de) auto	car
(de) avond	evening
(de) badjas	bathrobe
(de) badkamer	bathroom
(de) badkuip	bathtub
(de) bagage	luggage
(de) bak	storage bin
(de) banaan	banana
(de) bank	couch
(de) beek	brook
(de) behandeling	treatment

(de) berg	mountain
(de) bestemming	destination
(de) bevolkingsgroei	population growth
(de) bibliotheek	library
(de) bioscoop	cinema
(de) bleekselderij	celery
(de) bliksem	lightning
(de) bloem	flower, flour
(de) bloemkool	cauliflower
(de) bodem	bottom
(de) boekenkast	bookcase
(de) boerderij	farm
(de) boodschappen	groceries
(de) boodschappenlijst	shopping list
(de) bouwvakker	construction worker
(de) brandweer	firefighters
(de) brief	letter
(de) bril	pair of glasses
(de) broek	pants
(de) broer	brother
(de) buik	stomach
(de) buikpijn	stomachache
(de) bureaustoel	desk chair
(de) bus	bus
(de) buurt	neighborhood, vicinity
(de) chef	chef
(de) cursus	course
(de) dag	day
(de) dam	dam
(de) deur	door
(de) diepte	depth
(de) dochter	daughter

(de) documentaire	documentary
(de) dokter/arts	doctor/physician
(de) doperwt	pea
(de) douane	customs
(de) drank	(alcoholic) beverage
(de) druif	grape
(de) duim	thumb
(de) duizeligheid	dizziness
(de) duw	push
(de) eetkamer	dining room
(de) elektricien	electrician
(de) familie	family
(de) fauteuil	armchair
(de) fiets	bicycle, bike
(de) fles	bottle
(de) geboortedatum	birth date
(de) gil	scream
(de) gitaar	guitar
(de) graden	degrees
(de) groenten	vegetables
(de) hand	hand
(de) handbagage	hand luggage
(de) handdoek	towel
(de) handschoenen	gloves
(de) haven	port
(de) helm	helmet
(de) herfst, (het) najaar	fall
(de) heup	hip
(de) heuvel	hill
(de) hittegolf	ice
(de) hoed	hat
(de) hoek	corner

(de) hond	dog
(de) hoofdstraat	main street
(de) hoofdpijn	headache
(de) huid	skin
(de) huisarts	general practitioner
(de) huiskamer	living room
(de) incheckbalie	check-in counter
(de) ingenieur	engineer
(de) instapkaart	boarding pass
(de) jas	coat
(de) jurk	dress
(de) kaars	candle
(de) kaas	cheese
(de) kam	comb
(de) kamer	room
(de) kast	closet
(de) keelpijn	sore throat
(de) kers	cherry
(de) ketting	necklace
(de) keuken	kitchen
(de) keukenkastjes	kitchen cabinets
(de) kiespijn	toothache
(de) kilo	kilogram
(de) kinderen	children
(de) klachten	symptoms
(de) kleding	clothing
(de) kledingwinkel	clothing store
(de) kleren	clothes
(de) klerenkast	closet
(de) kleur	color
(de) knoflook	garlic
(de) koffer	suitcase

(de) kom	bowl
(de) komedie	comedy
(de) komkommer	cucumber
(de) koorts	fever
(de) korte broek	shorts
(de) kringloopwinkel	thrift shop
(de) kunstenaar, artiest	artist
(de) kussens	pillows, cushions
(de) kust	coast
(de) laarzen	boots
(de) lamp	lamp
(de) landingsbaan	landing strip
(de) leentermijn	loan term
(de) leeuw	lion
(de) lente, (het) voorjaar	spring
(de) leraar, lerares	teacher (m/f)
(de) les	lesson
(de) lip	lip
(de) long	lung
(de) luchtvaartmaatschappij	airline
(de) maaltijd	meal
(de) maan	moon
(de) magnetron	microwave
(de) mama	mom
(de) man	husband, man
(de) mandarijn	tangerine
(de) markt	market
(de) melk	milk
(de) meloen	melon
(de) meneer	man, Mr.
(de/het) mens	person, human being
(de) meubels	furniture

(de) mevrouw	lady, Mrs.
(de) middag	afternoon
(de) minuut	minute
(de) misdaadfilm	crime movie
(de) moeder	mother
(de) mond	mouth
(de) mouw	sleeve
(de) muziek	music
(de) nacht	night
(de) neef	cousin, nephew
(de) neus	nose
(de) nicht	cousin, niece
(de) nooduitgang	emergency exit
(de) ochtend	morning
(de) oma	grandmother
(de) omstandigheden	circumstances
(de) oom	uncle
(de) opa	grandfather
(de) open haard	fireplace
(de) oppervlakte	surface area
(de) ouders	parents
(de) pan	pan
(de) papa	dad
(de) passagier	passenger
(de) pauw	peacock
(de) peer	pear
(de) pen	pen
(de) perzik	peach
(de) pet	cap
(de) peuter	toddler
(de) pijnstiller	painkiller
(de) piloot	pilot

(de) pindakaas	peanut butter
(de) plank	shelf
(de) plek	place
(de) politicus	politician
(de) pop	doll
(de) pyjama	pajamas
(de) recensie	review
(de) regen	rain
(de) regenboog	rainbow
(de) regenjas	raincoat
(de) regisseur	director
(de) reiziger	traveler
(de) riem	seatbelt
(de) rivier	river
(de) rode bieten	beets
(de) rok	skirt
(de) rol	roll
(de) röntgenfoto	X-ray
(de) rug	back
(de) rugpijn	backache
(de) rugzak	backpack
(de) saus	sauce
(de) schoen	shoe
(de) scholier	student
(de) school	school
(de) schoonmaker	cleaner
(de) schouder	shoulder
(de) sinaasappel	orange
(de) sla	lettuce
(de) slaapkamer	bedroom
(de) slang	snake, hose
(de) sleutel	key

(de) sneeuw	snow
(de) snelheid	speed
(de) softwareontwikkelaar	software designer
(de) sok	sock
(de) spiegel	mirror
(de) spierpijn	sore muscle(s)
(de) spinazie	spinach
(de) sporthal	sports hall
(de) sportschoenen	sports shoes
(de) sportschool	gym
(de) spreekkamer	consultation room
(de) stad	city
(de) stem	voice, vote
(de) ster	star, celebrity
(de) steward(ess)	air host(ess)
(de) stip	dot
(de) stoel	chair
(de) stropdas	tie
(de) studeerkamer	study
(de) supermarkt	supermarket
(de) tafel	table
(de) tante	aunt
(de) tas	bag
(de) taxi	taxi
(de) teen	toe
(de) temperatuur	temperature
(de) timmerman	carpenter
(de) toilet	restroom
(de) tomaat	tomato
(de) tong	tongue
(de) tor	beetle
(de) tram	tram

(de) trein	train
(de) trui	sweater
(de) tuin	garden
(de) tussenstop	stopover
(de) ui	onion
(de) uitslag	rash, test results
(de) universiteit	university
(de) vader	father
(de) vallei	valley
(de) veiligheidscontrole	security check
(de) verf	paint
(de) verhoging	slight (body) temperature
(de) verpleegster	nurse
(de) vertaler	translator
(de) vertraging	delay
(de) vertrekhal	departure hall
(de) vinger	finger
(de) vis	fish
(de) vleugel	wings
(de) vlucht	flight
(de) voet	foot
(de) voetbaluitslag	football result
(de) voetganger	pedestrian
(de) vrachtauto / vrachtwagen	truck
(de) vriendin	female friend, girlfriend
(de) vrouw	wife, woman
(de) wasbak	sink
(de) wasmachine	washing machine
(de) waterval	waterfall
(de) wedstrijd	match, game
(de) week	week
(de) weg	road

(de) werknemer	employee
(de) wetenschapper	scientist
(de) winkel	shop
(de) winkel assistent	shop assistant
(de) winter	winter
(de) wintermaanden	winter months
(de) wiskunde	mathematics
(de) witte kool	white cabbage
(de) woestijn	desert
(de) wolk	cloud
(de) wortel	carrot, root
(de) zaal	hall
(de) zee	sea
(de) zomer	summer
(de) zomervakantie	summer vacation
(de) zon	sun
(de) zoon	son
(de) zorgen	worries
(de) zus	sister
(het) aantal	amount, number
(het) abonnement	subscription
(het) avondeten	dinner
(het) bed	bed
(het) been	leg
(het) begin	beginning
(het) beroep	profession
(het) blad	leaf
(het) boek	book
(het) boekingsnummer	booking number
(het) bord	plate, sign
(het) bos	forest
(het) bot	bone

(het) brood	bread
(het) bureau	desk
(het) cabinepersoneel	cabin crew
(het) centrum	center
(het) ei	egg
(het) eiland	island
(het) einde	end
(het) feest	party
(het) fornuis	stove
(het) geld	money
(het) gezicht	face
(het) glas	glass
(het) gordijn	curtain
(het) haar	hair
(het) hart	heart
(het) herenpak	men's suit
(het) huis	house
(het) inkomen	income
(het) ijs	heat wave
(het) joggingpak	jogging suit
(het) kaartje	ticket
(het) kantoor	office
(het) kind	child
(het) kleinkind	grandchild
(het) koekje	cookie
(het) kwartier	quarter
(het) lek	leak
(het) licht	light
(het) lid	member
(het) lidmaatschap	membership
(het) linkerbeen	left leg
(het) luisterboek	audiobook

(het) mandje	basket
(het) meer	lake
(het) meisje	girl
(het) menselijk lichaam	human body
(het) merk	brand
(het) nieuws	news
(het) onweer	thunderstorm
(het) oog	eye
(het) oor	ear
(het) openbaar vervoer	public transport
(het) pakket	package
(het) paspoort	passport
(het) plein	main square
(het) plafond	ceiling
(het) politiebureau	police station
(het) raam	window
(het) recept	prescription
(het) rechterbeen	right leg
(het) restaurant	restaurant
(het) riet	reed
(het) sap	juice
(het) schilderij	painting
(het) schip	ship
(het) seizoen	season
(het) overhemd	shirt
(het) sproetje	freckle
(het) stadhuis	town hall
(het) station	railway station
(het) stoelnummer	seat number
(het) strand	beach
(het) tijdschrift	magazine
(het) toetje	dessert

(het) touw	rope
(het) uur	hour
(het) verhaal	story
(het) verzoek	request
(het) visum	visa
(het) vlees	meat
(het) vliegticket	flight ticket
(het) vliegtuig	airplane
(het) vliegveld, (de) luchthaven	airport
(het) vuur	fire
(het) web	web
(het) weer	weather
(het) werk	work
(het) werkwoord	verb
(het) woordenboek	dictionary
(het) zalfje	ointment
(het) ziekenhuis	hospital
(het) zwembad	swimming pool
(het) badpak	swimsuit
's avonds	in the evening
's middags	in the afternoon
's nachts	at night
's ochtends, 's morgens	in the morning
aan de linkerkant	on the left-hand side
aan de rechterkant	on the right-hand side
aangenaam	it's a pleasure to meet you
aankomen	to arrive
aansteken	to light
aardig	friendly
ach	ah/oh well
acht	eight
achtentwintig	twenty-eight

achter	behind
achter elkaar	in a row
achthonderd	eight hundred
achttien	eighteen
afgesproken	agreed
afscheid nemen	to say goodbye
afwassen	to wash the dishes
al	already
alles	everything
als	if, when
altijd	always
Amerikaans	American
april	April
Argentijns	Argentinian
Argentinië	Argentina
augustus	August
Australië	Australia
Australisch	Australian
Braziliaans	Brazilian
Brazilië	Brazil
bah	yuck
bedankt	thanks
beginnen	to start
begrijpen	to understand
behalve	except
bekend	well-known
beloven	to promise
ben	am
besmettelijk	contagious
bestellen	to order
betalen	to pay
bewegen	to move

bewolkt	cloudy
bezoeken	to visit
bezorgd	worried
bijten	to bite
bijvoorbeeld	for example
biljard	quadrillion
biljoen	trillion
binnenkomen	to enter
blauw	blue
boarden	to board
branden	to burn
brengen	to bring
Brits	British
bruin	brown
Canadees	Canadian
Chinees	Chinese
Colombiaans	Colombian
daar	there
daarom	therefore
dansen	to dance
dat	that
de	the
De Verenigde Staten	The United States
december	December
Deens	Danish
Denemarken	Denmark
depressief	depressed
dertien	thirteen
dertig	thirty
deze	this, these
dichtbij	close (to)
die	that, those

dinsdag	Tuesday
dit	this
doei, doeg	bye
doen	to do
dol zijn op	to adore somebody, something
donderdag	Thursday
donker	dark
dood	dead
draaien	to turn, to play a movie
dragen	to carry, to wear
dramatisch	dramatic
drie	three
drieëndertig	thirty-three
drieëntwintig	twenty-three
driehonderd	three hundred
droog	dry
drukken	to press
Duits	German
Duitsland	Germany
duizelig	dizzy
duizend	thousand
duur	expensive
een	a/an
één	one
een beetje	a little bit
eenendertig	thirty-one
eenentwintig	twenty-one
elf	elf
elk	each
emotioneel	emotional
en	and
eng	scary

er is	there is
er zijn	there are
erg	very, awful
erger worden	to get worse
ernstig	severe
februari	February
fel	bright (color)
fietsen	to cycle, to bike
fijn	nice
fijne dag	(have a) nice day
Frankrijk	France
Frans	French
gaaf	great
gaan	to go
gebroken	broken
gebruiken	to use
gedeeltelijk	partially
geel	yellow
geen	no
gefeliciteerd	congratulations
gek	crazy
gelden	to be valid
geloven	to believe
gemiddeld	average
genoeg	enough
gesloten	closed
gestrest	stressed
getrouwd	married
geven	to give
geweldig	awesome
gewoon	simply
gids	tour guide

gisteren	yesterday
goededag	good day
goedemiddag	good afternoon
goedemorgen	good morning
goedenavond	good evening
goedkoop	cheap
goh	gosh
graag	preferably
grappig	funny
grijs	gray
groen	green
groot	big
Groot-Brittannië	Great Britain
half	half
hallo	hello
hard	hard, loudly
hardrennen	to go jogging
hartelijk bedankt	thank you very much
hartig	savory
he he	finally!
hebben	to have
heerlijk	delicious
heet	hot
helaas	unfortunately
helemaal niet	not at all
het	it, the
hetzelfde	the same
hier	here
hierop	on this
hij	he
hoe	how
hoeveel	how much/many

hoewel	although
hoi	hi
honderd	hundred
hoog	high
hoogste	highest
houden	to hold
houden van	to love
houten	wooden
huidig	current
huilen	to cry
ieder	each, every
ik	I
in	in(side)
in de gaten houden	to keep an eye on it
inchecken	to check in
inderdaad	exactly
innemen	to ingest
inrichten	to decorate
instappen	to get in
interessant	interesting
ja	yes
januari	January
Japans	Japanese
jeetje	gosh
jeuken	to itch
jij/je	you (singular)
joh	of course
jouw	your
juli	July
jullie	you (plural)
juni	June
kieskeurig	picky

kijken	to look
klein	small
kleuren	to color in
kloppen	to be correct, to knock
koel	cool
komen	to come
kopen	to buy
kort	short
kosten	to cost
koud	cold
krijgen	to receive
kunnen	to be able to
laag	low
landen	to land
lang	long
langs	past
last hebben van	to suffer from, to be bothered by
leggen	to put
lekker	tasty
lekker vinden	to like (food)
lelijk	ugly
lenen	to lend
leren	to learn
leuk	fun
leven	to live
licht	light
lief	sweet
liggen	to lie, to be located
links	left
lopen	to walk
luisteren	to listen
maandag	Monday

maandelijks	montly
maar	but
maart	March
Marokkaans	Moroccan
Marokko	Morocco
meebrengen	to bring along
meerdere	multiple
meervoud	plural
meestal	usually
meevallen	to not be that bad
mei	May
menen	to mean
menig	many
meteen	right away
Mexicaans	Mexican
Mexico	Mexico
miljard	billion
miljoen	million
misschien	maybe
misselijk	nauseous
missen	to miss
mistig	foggy
modern	modern
moe	tired
moeilijk	difficult
moeten	to have to
mogen	to be allowed to
mooi	pretty
morgen	tomorrow
naam	name
naar	unpleasant
naast	next to

nadat	after
nadenken	to think about
natuurlijk	of course
Nederland	The Netherlands
Nederlands	Dutch
neem	take
negen	nine
negenentwintig	twenty-nine
negenhonderd	nine hundred
negentien	nineteen
negentig	ninety
nemen	to take
niet	not
niet hoeven	to not have an obligation
nog	still
nooit	never
nou	well
nou zeg	geez
november	November
nu	now
nu	now that
nul	zero
oefenen	to practice
oei	oof
Oekraïens	Ukrainian
Oekraïne	Ukraine
of	or, whether
oh jee	uh oh
oktober	October
omdat	because
onder	under
ontzettend	incredibly

onweren	thunderstorms
ook	also
op	on
opbellen	to call on the phone
ophalen	to pick up
ophangen	to end a phonecall, to hang up
opletten	to pay attention
oplopen	increase
opruimen	to tidy
opstijgen	to take off
oranje	orange (color)
ouderwets	old-fashioned
overgaan	pass
paars	purple
parkeren	to park
per stuk	per unit
pijnlijk	painful
pittig	spicy
plukken	to pick
prachtig	beautiful
proberen	to try
publiceren	to publish
raar	weird
rechtdoor	straight ahead
rechts	right
redden	to save
regenen	to rain
reizen	to travel
rennen	to run
rijden	to drive
roken	to smoke
romantisch	romantic

rood	red
roze	pink
Rusland	Russia
Russisch	Russian
saai	boring
samenwerken	to collaborate
schoon	clean
schoonmaken	to clean
september	September
sla af	turn
sla links af	turn left
sla rechts af	turn right
slaan	to hit
slapen	to sleep
slecht	bad
smal	narrow
sneeuwen	to snow
snel	fast
soms	sometimes
Spaans	Spanish
Spanje	Spain
spannend	exciting, thrilling
spreken	to speak
staan	to stand
stad	city
stil	quiet
strak	tight
studeren	to study
stuk	broken
sturen	to steer
tachtig	eighty
tegenover	opposite

tekenen	to draw
terugbrengen	to return
terwijl	while
testen	to test
thuis	at home
tien	ten
tijdens	during
tjonge jonge	well, well
toen	when
top	excellent
tot	until
tot ziens	bye
totaan	until
totdat	until
triljoen	quintillion
twaalf	twelve
twee	two
tweeduizend	two thousand
tweeëndertig	thirty-two
tweeëntwintig	twenty-two
tweehonderd	two hundred
twintig	twenty
u	you (singular and plural, formal)
uitleggen	to explain
uitproberen	to try out
uitstappen	to disembark
vaak	often
vanavond	this evening
vandaag	today
vanmiddag	this afternoon
vannacht	tonight/last night

vanochtend, vanmorgen	this morning
veel	a lot (of)
veertien	fourteen
veertig	forty
ver	far
veranderen	change
verbinden	to connect
verdwaald	lost
vergeten	to forget
verhuizen	to move
verkopen	to sell
verlengen	to extend
vers	fresh
verslaan	to defeat
vertellen	to tell
vertrekken	to leave
verven	to paint
verzwikken	sprain
vier	four
vierentwintig	twenty-four
vierhonderd	four hundred
vies	dirty
vijf	five
vijfentwintig	twenty-five
vijfhonderd	five hundred
vijftien	fifteen
vijftig	fifty
vijfentwintig	twenty-five
vijfhonderd	five hundred
vijftien	fifteen
vijftig	fifty
voetballen	to play football

vol	full
voor	for
vooral	mainly
voordat	before
voorschrijven	to prescribe
voorstellen	to imagine, propose, introduce someone
vragen	to ask
vriezen	to be below freezing
vrijdag	Friday
waaien	to blow (wind)
waar	where, true
waarheen	where to
waarom	why
wandelen	to walk, to hike
wanneer	when
wat	what
we (wij)	we
weggaan	to go away
wegzetten	to put away
weinig	few
welk(e)	which
werken	to work
weten	to know
wie	who
wijd	wide
willen	to want
wisselvallig	changeable (weather)
wit	white
woensdag	Wednesday
wonen	to live
worden	to become
zaterdag	Saturday

ze (zij)	she, they, them
zelfstandig naamwoord	noun
zes	six
zesentwintig	twenty-six
zeshonderd	six hundred
zestien	sixteen
zestig	sixty
zetten	to put
zeuren	to whine
zeven	seven
zevenentwintig	twenty-seven
zevenhonderd	seven hundred
zeventien	seventeen
zeventig	seventy
zich gedragen	to behave
zich haasten	to hurry
zich herinneren	to remember
zich niet lekker voelen	to feel unwell
zich schamen	to be ashamed/embarrassed
zich verbazen	to be amazed, to be surprised
zich vergissen	to make a mistake
zich vermaken	to have fun
zich verslapen	to oversleep
zich vervelen	to be bored
zich voelen	to feel
zich zorgen maken	to worry
zien	to see
zijn	to be
zilveren	silver
zitten	to sit, to be located
zo zo	well, well
zoals	as soon as

zodra	as soon as
zoeken	to look for
zoet	sweet
zo'n	such a
zondag	Sunday
zonnig	sunny
zout	salt
Zuid-Afrika	South Africa
Zuid-Afrikaans	South African
zulk	such
zwanger	pregnant
zwart	black
Zweden	Sweden
Zweeds	Swedish
zwemmen	to swim

CONCLUSION

Well done, you have completed our Dutch vocabulary workbook! You have acquired an enormous amount of useful vocabulary and grammar in the process, and we hope this progress has inspired you to keep on studying.

Now it is your turn to continue on your learning journey with other resources! Remember that Lingo Mastery has plenty more content and books in Dutch for you to continue building your knowledge of the language.

And just to make sure you can keep on improving your Dutch and feel more confident about your capabilities, here are a few suggestions:

1. Do not feel disappointed if you are not that fluent yet. Learning a new language takes **time** and, most importantly, a lot of **practice**! Don't lose the motivation you've been building and enjoy the challenges of the language. You can do it!

2. **Celebrate** every single one of your accomplishments, no matter how small they are. Were you able to understand a whole video in Dutch or maybe just a part of it? Did you pronounce a few sentences correctly? Did you remember some useful vocabulary? These are all reasons to celebrate!

3. Use all the **resources** that you can find in order to improve your knowledge. Movies, podcasts, songs, TV series, short videos online, everything is useful!

4. It's also very important to connect with language that's useful for your **context and interests:** make sure to focus on finding resources about topics that you need or are interested in, because this is the best way to build a personal connection to the Dutch language, and it will also increase your motivation to keep studying.

5. Make use of every opportunity you have to talk to someone in Dutch, and **don't be afraid** of making mistakes. Mistakes are a normal—and very useful—part of the learning process.

6. Most importantly: **have fun!**

MORE BOOKS BY LINGO MASTERY

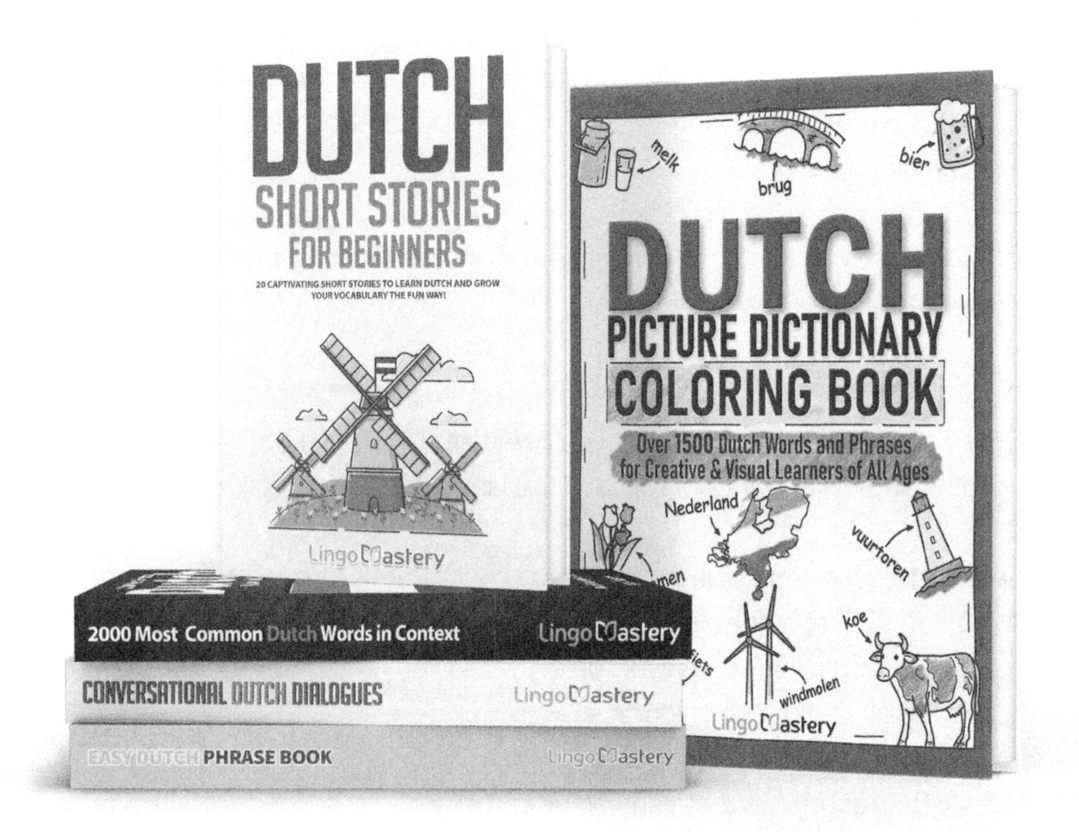

We are not done teaching you Dutch until you're fluent!

Here are some other titles you might find useful in your journey of mastering Dutch:

✓ Dutch Short Stories for Beginners

✓ Intermediate Dutch Short Stories

✓ 2000 Most Common Dutch Words in Context

✓ Conversational Dutch Dialogues

But we got many more!

Check out all of our titles at **www.LingoMastery.com/Dutch**

Printed in Great Britain
by Amazon